CROSSCOURT

JAIDIP MUKERJEA
with Papri Sen Sri Raman

Vitasta

Published by
Renu Kaul Verma
Vitasta Publishing Pvt Ltd
2/15, Ansari Road, Daryaganj
New Delhi – 110 002
info@vitastapublishing.com

ISBN 978-81-960413-0-4
© Jaidip Mukerjea
First Edition 2023
MRP ₹495

Cover and layout by Somesh Kumar Mishra
Printed by Chaman Enterprises, New Delhi

To
Baba
ADHIP MUKERJEA
& Maa ADITI
For finding that spark and
deeming me worthy not
only as son but
as a student at the
feet of Hermes

Aditi and Adhip Mukerjea (fourth and fifth from the right; standing) with family members at a reception for then Governor of West Bengal, Kailash Nath Katju (seated, centre).

On the left is grandmother Usha Mukerjea and on the right is aunt, Justice
Manjula Bose, one of the first woman judges of Kolkata High Court.

Jaidip Mukerjea with mother Aditi (left) and wife Sharmin.

Contents

Women at Kolkata's tennis courts in the 1930s and '40s.

A Word on Writing of this Book

Sharmin Mukerjea
Chairperson JMTA

I often wondered why a famous sports person like Jaidip Mukerjea did not think of writing his life's story earlier.

When I first met Jaidip in 1996, he was Team India's Davis Cup Captain. The transition from friend to wife gave me a greater opportunity to look closely at a glorious family history of the pre-independence era; to discover not only the loving husband but the kind and courteous person Jaidip is; and to find to my horror as a media professional that he is all sports and with few words.

For twenty-seven years, I have been asking him to write about his affair with the Davis Cup, the romance of the game, the glamour on the court, the warmth of the limelight. At 80, finally, I have managed to convince Jaidip to pen the story of his foray in the world of tennis. On his part, it has been a Herculean effort for the last several years; nevertheless, slowly but surely, writing bit by bit, a chronicle of the making of an ace sportsman has emerged. It is also a history of an era – a tale of transition from Raj India to a nation state that plays under its own banner. This is my gift to his fans, admirers, to tennis in India and all our readers.

Sharmin Mukerjea

The Gentleman Team Player

Ramanathan Krishnan
Tennis player

I first saw Jaidip, not in Calcutta but in Allahabad, in the nineteen fifties.

He was a 15-year-old boy, five years younger to me, and had come to play in the junior event. I watched him for a few minutes along with the other juniors. He impressed me with his style of play – aggressive, more on the unorthodox side – which is a strong point in tennis, and keen to play in the forecourt, which was grass court-style tennis in those days.

I felt happy seeing him for selfish reasons. I was keen to do well in the Davis Cup competition for India. At that time, Naresh Kumar and I were the two-men team. I knew we needed at least five or six players to perform well in Davis Cup, as that would give us choice on different playing surfaces and against various opponents.

My dream came true in 1966, nearly ten years later, when we reached the Challenge Round finals against Australia. Jaidip and I teamed up to beat Germany and Brazil. And in the Challenge Round, registered a win against the Australians, Newcombe and Roche in the Doubles. They were practically unbeaten, having won all Grand Slam events and many other tournaments, too. This victory is considered the best in the Doubles for an Indian pair, and Jaidip's performance had been unparalleled. Whenever we lost a vital point in a big match, Jaidip always charged back and this was his main asset.

For camaraderie and performance level, our 1966 team, consisting of Jaidip, Premjit Lall, S P Misra and Ramanathan Krishnan, was according to many the best ever team to represent India. Our behaviour on and off the court was taken into consideration.

If I reached the singles semi-finals of Wimbledon twice, Jaidip has the unique record of reaching the last sixteen of every Grand Slam – Wimbledon, French, Australian and Forest Hills (USA). This is an outstanding achievement, which shows that he could play on any surface under different conditions.

Finally, during tournament play with him for more than ten years at least, I never saw him 'steal' a point on the court! It was, therefore, a pleasure playing with him in a team.

Ramanathan Krishnan

Tennis is My Life

Jaidip Mukerjea
The Tennis player author

As I sit down to pen my life's journey, the belief that I owe it all to Tennis grips me more firmly than ever before.

The game has taken me all over the world as a tennis player, coach, administrator and has brought me in touch with many incredible people. They range from tennis players to business magnates, actors to politicians. Even some, whose names may have never appeared in the columns of any newspaper but whose names are etched in my heart in very fine letters. Many of them have become lifelong friends and many have helped me to shape my hopes, thoughts and dreams.

My little contribution to Indian tennis has been as a player, captain, coach who has had the opportunity to represent my country as an unofficial ambassador for Indian tennis.

Looking back, I now think it is appropriate to share my life experiences with the new generation and sports lovers. I feel the young generation of our country should know more about the hard work that Indian tennis players of yesteryear such as Ramanathan Krishnan, Premjit Lall and Jaidip Mukerjea – the original Three Musketeers of Indian tennis – put in which took India to the Davis Cup finals for the first time in 1966.

I had been contemplating writing my memories ever since I partially retired from tennis, but one thing or the other always crept up. All these many long years, it was the game that kept me tied to it with silk threads and I could never manage Time.

Finally, during the Covid pandemic when we were all under lockdown, my wife Sharmin inspired me to pen my thoughts about my life and times and that's how it all started. Without her support, inspiration and encouragement this book would not have been possible.

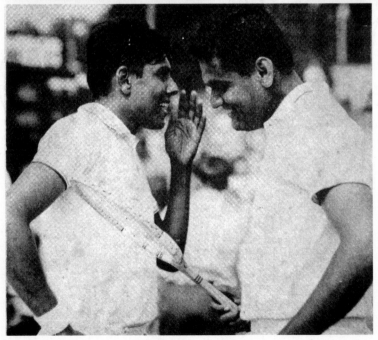

Chapter 1

ALL IN THE GENES PERHAPS

I REMEMBER ONCE, when I was very young, I was told by my mother Aditi that a big man will be coming to our house to meet Basanti Devi, my great-grandmother. The man was none other than Mahatma Gandhi.

Though I lived with my parents on Theatre Road (now Shakespeare Sarani), my young wondrous mind used to constantly wander across the skies of 5, Nafar Kundu Road, longing to join Shuma, Gopali and Molin for a session of kite flying.

On Nafar Kundu Road lived my maternal great-grandmother Basanti Devi, whom I used to lovingly call 'Mamaa'. As Deshbandhu Chittaranjan Das was one of the tallest leaders of the Swadeshi Movement, Gandhiji came to pay his respect to his wife, Basanti Devi whenever he visited Kolkata in the 1940s.

The Deshbandhu with Basanti Devi.

Basanti was a steadfast woman, strong in her own convictions. Following her husband's death in 1925, she had continued with many of his nation-building initiatives, especially those related to women's upliftment. Overcoming her great loss, with a lot of courage and grit she managed to curve out her own space as a philanthropist, nationalist and advocate of women's rights in her own way. Fortunately, Dr B C Roy, the first Chief Minister of West Bengal, and other eminent Bengalis helped Basanti Devi to buy a house in Nafar Kundu Road in Bhawanipore. Thus, this was a place where many a great mind met and discussed affairs related to her endeavours and well-being.

One particular instance in this house that is etched in my memory is the visit of the 'Big Man'. The day saw me as a child of four or five, being dressed and packed, along with my mother, from our Theatre Road residence to Mamaa's house early in the morning. Our presence was required to oversee the comfort of the visitor. On the way, I was repeatedly warned to be on my best behaviour. Much to my dismay, on reaching Mamaa's house, the usual warmth bestowed on me by the household was missing and the whole house seemed to be more in a fire-fighting mode, trying to put everything in order, to welcome the Big Man.

It was probably at around noon that we all stood outside the collapsible gates which led to the pathway across the lawn to the ground floor and the big living room of the house, where all arrangements were made to welcome our honoured guest.

When I saw him, I exclaimed to my mother, 'You told me

that a big man is coming but this person is a small man'.

A crowd of friends and relatives had gathered to see the Mahatma. As Gandhiji entered our main gate and was crossing the lawn before it, he heard my remark and smiled and told me, 'Yes Beta… my son, you are right… I am a small man'. The child's eye measured the man by height, expecting a giant. The Mahatma, in his generous manner, had never claimed to be a great man or a saint; he had always said, he was an *aam aadmi*, a common man, an ordinary man and he chose to adopt my 'small man' remark in that sense. My mother and grandmother were very upset.

Later that day, playfully, I hid Gandhiji's *kharam* (wooden footwear, the Indian clog, *kharaoo*) which I finally brought back from the secret hideout and gave it back to the Big Man. That was adding insult to injury. The Mahatma proved his greatness once again by blessing me and saying, 'This child will one day make us all proud'. My mother had had enough of my bad behaviour. That day, for the first time, she thrashed me.

My family's tryst with embarrassment did not end there. Again, a few months later, I accompanied my mother and Mamaa (Basanti Devi) to Gandhiji's ashram in Barrackpore, where and when Mamaa and my mother were discussing serious matters relating to the nation and its people, I happened to be merrily soiling my pants. After which, my family decided to keep me as far away as possible from Gandhiji, even though he was very much in touch with Mamaa till the very end of his life.

MY GREAT-GRANDFATHER C R Das was an associate of Moti Lal Nehru, and had started a political party called Swarajya Party to facilitate the freedom of India from British rule. He was an activist lawyer, involved with the Anushilan Samiti, and an advocate for Rishi Aurobindo, his brother Barin Ghosh and a host of other young Bengal revolutionaries implicated in the infamous Alipore conspiracy case (1909-10) when the colonial rulers alleged, the nationalists were making bombs. They were so afraid of these young nationalists that they moved the Raj capital away in 1912 from Kolkata, then Calcutta, to Delhi, the Mughal capital.

Basanti Devi, my great-grandmother and 'The Iron Lady' of my maternal family, has always been a deep influence in my life. I would now like to take you to 1946 and share an incident involving her, which speaks volumes about her character and persona. The incident used to be narrated to me during my infancy by my mother like a folklore to instil fear in me, so that I would go to bed early, much to her relief.

As I have seen, my Mamaa's house was always filled with visitors from various walks of life. The place had become a melting pot of culture, religion and ideas. People came to seek her blessings, solicit advice and discuss various issues. Mamaa would always welcome them with a smile and serve them endless cups of tea, along with lip-smacking savouries and other kinds of dishes.

Both Basanti Devi and her daughter-in-law Sujata were great cooks but were vegetarians as in those days, widows were not allowed to eat non-veg food. Though she become a vegetarian after the death of her husband, but keeping her mind, heart and hearth open, Basanti Devi had also employed a *Khansama*, a male cook named Afsar, who specialised in preparing Mughlai dishes for her family (including me and I used to love the food prepared by him) and her guests.

As such, neither my maternal, nor my paternal family put any kind of religion into me. They never put any pressure on me to go to Saraswati Pujo and Durga Pujo. This I did later, with my friends. My father was all Cambridge food, and we had ham and eggs with umm… sausages at home. And we had beef steaks and a lot of Western cultural influences. However,

I was never forced to do anything or like anything or dislike anything.

Now, many of you must be aware that the months leading to India's Independence from the British Raj and even few months subsequently, saw the country in much upheaval. This was due to the tension that arose between two religious communities as the decision regarding 'Partition of India' was taken on religious lines. Mamaa was very upset at that time with the nation's state of affairs and particularly about Afsar, as he belonged to a community whose presence was negligible in the area in Kolkata where Mamaa's house was situated.

As Mamaa had foreseen, her apprehension regarding Afsar's safety turned out to be true and one night an angry mob quite literally barged into her house, looking for Afsar, possibly not knowing whose house they had stepped into. The gang of armed men were hardly prepared for the rude shock that followed.

Like always, Mamaa took charge of the situation herself and confronted the angry, misguided men, with a strong message – that they would have to walk over her dead body in order to even touch Afsar. The mob had most likely never confronted a matriarch of such exemplary courage and valour and backed out, only leaving behind a message that they would again come back. But that never happened.

When I was a little older and was able to grasp the gravity of the situation, I asked her about the emotions which ran through her during the confrontation. Was she afraid, I asked. She told me, yes, she did fear but the fear was overshadowed by the conviction and love that she possessed for her family and the ethos of her motherland that gave her syncretic beliefs and taught her non-violence.

Another incident which comes to my mind was from the Partition year, 1947. We lived in Theatre Road and I was about five years old. You know the Rawdon Street-Theatre Road crossing, and the International Club at that corner. It was a dark winter evening, and looking out of the window, I saw this guy cycling right in front of our house. Someone slashed him with a blade. The man's cycle tottered and fell. This incident from childhood has really stuck in my mind.

Chittaranjan Das with cane in hand, and Mahatma Gandhi on the Hill Cart Road near Kakjhora, Darjeeling in 1925.

MY MOTHER WAS the eldest granddaughter of Chittaranjan Das and her father was Chiroranjan Das, the Deshbandhu's only son who unfortunately passed away at the young age of twenty-seven, leaving behind his young wife Sujata and three young daughters, Aditi, Swarupa and Indrani.

When Chiroranjan died, my mother was four years old, Swarupa was two and Indrani was only a year old.

It was a very hard and tough time for all of them as Deshbandhu (November 1870-June 1925) had given away all his property to charity to raise funds for the freedom struggle. The family did not have a roof over their head at first. My great-grandmother and my grandmother, Sujata Devi, brought up the three girls in great hardship.

Aditi, my mother.

My grandmother Sujata Devi was a very simple and soft person and the boss of her household was naturally Basanti Devi, who ran the house with an iron hand, in spite of losing her husband and son within a year. Another tragedy happened to the family when my youngest aunt, Indrani, passed away due to typhoid which was a deadly disease in those days; in fact, my mother and my aunt, both had typhoid. My mother survived but my aunt did not make it. I was very close to both my great-grandmother and grandmother and they both encouraged me to play and excel in sports.

When I won the Asian title for the first time in 1966, the first person I went to visit was my great-grandmother Basanti Devi (March 1880-May 1974). She was really pleased to see me, even though she was not very well at the time. The Basanti Devi Girls College in Kolkata is named after her.

My grandmother Sujata Devi had lost her husband at 23, and she devoted her life and soul to charity and to helping the poor. She started the Sujata Devi boarding school in Hazra, Kolkata which is still doing very well. She also started a school in Kalikapur, in South 24 Parganas. After Deshbandhu, Sujata took up her father-in-law's mantle and became a friend of the people. I used to accompany her on her trips to Kalikapur very often and liked to be with her a lot.

I LIVED WITH my parents, Adhip and Aditi Mukerjea along with my paternal grandfather, J C Mukerjea, at the junction of Theatre Road and Rawdon Street. Dadu, Jyotish Chandra Mukerjea, was a former president of the Board of Control for Cricket in India or BCCI and the first Bengali to hold this position. He was the person in my family from whom I have learnt what the word 'dedication' means.

Dadu was brought up in Bhagalpur, now in Bihar and belonged to an illustrious Brahmo family. After obtaining a degree in law, he decided to join the Civil Service under the British regime and rose to the position of a Senior Commissioner in the Kolkata (then, Calcutta) Municipal Corporation – a prized-position for any Indian in pre-independent India.

Initially we lived with my grandparents, first in Camac Street (now Abanindranath Sarani) where I was born, then in Theatre Road and finally in 6 Middleton Street. Though my grandfather was the chief executive of the Kolkata Corporation, he never thought of investing in houses and property but he helped a lot of people to do so. Once, he was offered a bungalow in Mandeville Gardens, Kolkata, which he rejected saying, who is going to live in a jungle? Little did he know it is today a prime property in Kolkata. In spite of being a very senior executive of Calcutta Corporation and later the town of Jamshedpur, J C Mukerjea refrained from buying any property for himself or his family members in order to ensure that words like 'nepotism,' 'favouritism' or 'opportunism' stay miles away from him. Like him, my father too had no interest in property.

When J C Mukerjea retired from his government job, he was soon roped in by the Tatas, to take care of the then newly-coming up steel town of Jamshedpur as its Chief Town Administrator. Office was always his second home and for him, work was worship.

When I was born as his first grandchild on 21 April 1942, in Kolkata, Dadu was posted in Jamshedpur, with a very busy work schedule. Despite all odds, he managed to reach Kolkata, taking the first train of the day from Jamshedpur, just to leave his beloved grandson with a gift of a 'Guinea,' a coin, minted in Great Britain between 1663 and 1814, that contained approximately one-quarter of an ounce of gold. He caught the night train back to Jamshedpur, so that he could start work again, the very next morning.

My father's mother, my grandmother Usha Mukerjea, was a prim and proper Bengali lady and a very good housewife. She had four children. The eldest was Gita, my Boropishi, then came my father Adhip, followed by another brother Pratip who died early. I do not know much about this uncle except that I have been told he was very fond of me. He died of Malaria in Sylhet which is now in Bangladesh.

The last of the siblings was Kobita pishi who is still going strong at the ripe age of 92.

My Chotopishi Kobita is only eleven years older and as such has been very close to me. We used to always argue and

My beautiful aunt Kobita.

fight all the time, she was very effective and won mostly in all our arguments. All the guys were crazy about her and when she went out with someone, she would always take me along as a stepney or insurance, as then when she got back, she could tell her father that, 'I took Jaidip for a long walk'. My Chotopishi finally settled down after rejecting many suitors and married a wonderful man named Tapan Sen who had two sons Rajesh and Anamit. I visit her as often as I can but due to the Covid situation, now I can no longer make it as often as I would like to. It was very hard for her when her son passed away.

We all lived together in Middleton Street. I used to go on long tram rides with my grandmother Usha, to places like Tollygunge, Ballygunge, Shyambazaar etc which I really enjoyed those days. For a child, it was like travelling on a mini train, like children today feel travelling on the fast metros and vista domes. Trams were fuller in the 1950s and it was a great way to travel in the city.

Grandmother Usha's younger sister, Burithakuma, Sudha Ray, was a very good and keen tennis player and used to play at the Calcutta Club every evening in a saree. In fact, she is the first woman in my family who went to the Calcutta Club to play tennis. Today I can proudly say that because of her, I at first began to learn to play tennis.

My Boropishi, Gita Mallick, was married to a very senior Eastern Railways officer and they used to take me on tour, travelling to Puri, Ranchi and other places by the salon carriage available for officials those days. It was great fun to travel by the salon car, it was like a home away from home, no booking and nothing to do, just go in the train and enjoy the scenery. Our own room and bathroom etc... travelling in the salon was really awesome.

THE TWENTIETH OF April 2022 was my mother's hundred and first birthday. She nearly died of typhoid when she was five. Thankfully, she has crossed the corona pandemic safely. I spoke to her in the morning and wished her and I felt the emotion in her voice. She was really happy to hear from her eldest son. Unfortunately, after the pandemic lockdown, I have not been able to see her much but I hope, now that we have learnt more about the virus and the world-wide illness, I will have the opportunity to visit her more often.

I really love her lunches when she cooks my favourite food – basically, mutton curry, *bandhakopi* (cabbage), greens (*sag*) etc. She is very active and she loves to walk around; she is frail but strong, perhaps she inherited her grandmother, Basanti Devi's magic genes.

My mother Aditi was lovingly called Minu by her close family and friends. She has always been an epitome of strength, my secret weapon, which has helped me win a lot of matches on court and a lot many battles off it.

Aditi did her schooling from Loreto House (Kolkata), commuting to school every day with her 'Best Friend and Cousin,' Siddhartha Shankar Ray (1920-2010), who used to study in St Xavier's Collegiate School, situated just a few blocks away from her school. Ray went on to become a former Union Minister of Education and then the Chief Minister of West

Bengal, also the Governor of Punjab and India's Ambassador to the United States. My mother was patient like her grandmother, but I was a child who provoked the family's patience.

One day, I was balancing myself on the parapet of the second floor veranda of my great-grandmother and grandmother's house and if I fell, I would fall in the garden twenty-five feet below. I was about eight years old. Neighbours from across the street saw me and telephoned my mother to sound an alert, 'Minudi, dekho tomar Jaidip ki korche....,' which meant Minu see what Jaidip is doing. Quickly, without making any noise, my mother came up behind me and caught me and brought me down. She then proceeded to spank me soundly. This was the second time that she beat me. I shudder to think now, had I fallen in the garden, India would never have seen Jaidip Mukerjea as a tennis player.

Though she was a very dutiful mother, she never came in between any decisions that I took, in the course of my life, be it, personal or professional. She practiced this philosophy, as she believed that she had instilled enough discipline and strength in her son, so that he could make his own decisions and take responsibility for them, too. She always preferred to remain in the background, providing comfort and stability to the family.

Only once in my entire tennis career did she come to the stands, to watch me play. The occasion happened to be at the Calcutta South Club. That day in 1966, I defeated Ramanathan Krishnan to lift the Asian Championships. But I always know, her blessings are always with me, whether she is far away or close by.

ADHIP MUKERJEA OR Baba (as we Bengalis call our fathers) perhaps has had the greatest influence in shaping me into a professional tennis player.

My dad was a very good sportsman and excelled in most outdoor games like cricket, football (soccer as the Americans call it), hockey and tennis. After schooling in St Xavier's College, Kolkata he went to study in England to Cambridge University's prestigious Claire College, where he won the tennis and hockey Blues. He had several job offers in England but he wanted to be close to his friends and family in Kolkata.

My father was the hockey captain of Mohun Bagan Football Club First Eleven and was responsible for taking the FC hockey team to the Aga Khan Trophy, a famous tournament in Bombay. His team stayed at the Taj Mahal hotel, as my father had many contacts and all the players who won and his friends there were very happy and excited, because in those days most Indian teams and players were housed in camps.

After returning from England to Kolkata, my father joined the Calcutta Tramways and worked with the tram company for a few years. Later he became the Director of Operations for the West Bengal State Transport Corporation which he had started. Baba, along with a handful of equally dedicated personnel, proved to be the backbone of this fast-expanding sector, making Calcutta State Transport Corporation a grand

Adhip and Aditi Mukerjea.

success in its initial years; its service extended to all corners of West Bengal.

Baba was a man of impeccable integrity, both in his professional and personal life. Though he started his working life with Calcutta Tramways, he was hand-picked by none other than the then Chief Minister of West Bengal, Dr Bidhan Chandra Roy (1882-1962), to play a leading role in the Human Resource Department of the Calcutta State Transport Corporation, when the organisation was absolutely in its nascent stage.

As he was in the Human Resource Department, he was instrumental in recruiting and appointing thousands of individuals in different capacities in the organisation, but always on the basis of merit, a trait which I cherish and seek to follow even today.

As far as I recall, Burithakuma, my grandmother's sister, first put a tennis racquet in my hand. My aunt Kobita too played tennis. So, my first understanding of the game that was to become my lifetime passion came from the versatile women in my family.

Dr Bidhan Chandra Roy

Chapter 2

——◦——

COURTING FAME
AT LA MARTINIERE

I JOINED LA MARTINIERE in 1950 at the age of eight and finished my senior Cambridge in December 1959. I think my name is still there on the school steps. We had a Prefect's Room and people would write their names on the steps there.

When I joined school, there were very few Indian boys in the school, most of the students were Anglo Indians, Armenians and British. It was a tough boys' school and one had to take care of one's self to survive here. Being talented at sports helped and I was popular with the students and the teachers.

The school encouraged students to take part in Boxing, Rugby and other games. The school had Past Students vs Present Students matches at La Martiniere and after the matches, we would get shandy (a beer cocktail) from the old boys.

We had a girls' school next door and Socials took place between the senior students of both, the boys' and girls' schools, frequently. This is where I learnt my ball room dancing. It became an asset later on in my life.

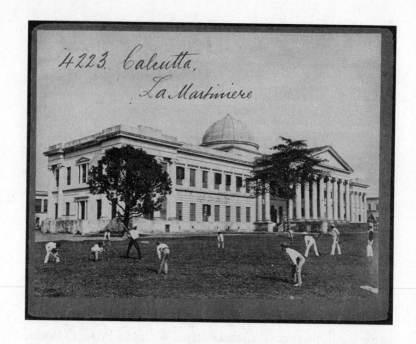

We used to have a swimming pool and we had a very good bunch of teachers who lived on the campus. I have some very happy and nostalgic memories of my school days.

We had some great teachers at school who were very broad-minded and were more like elder brothers than teachers. Some who come to my mind are Mr Peterson, Mr Maiden and Mr Fitzgerald and, of course, our principal at that time, Mr Harry Chalke who was very strict but very soft at heart.

I still remember in my senior Cambridge year (1959), I was selected to represent India at Wimbledon. As I was not a very good student, my father did not want me to go but our principal Mr Chalke convinced him to let me go and play, and assured my father that the school would provide me extra tuition, free of charge so that I could pass the board exam quite easily.

Mr Chalke migrated to the UK in 1960 and I used to invite him to watch Wimbledon every year from 1960 till he passed away in the early '70s.

Greg Fitzgerald, the son of Mr Fitzgerald, our maths teacher and house master, became a very good friend. He now lives in Sydney, Australia. In one of my trips to Sydney, Greg took me to meet his father, Mr Fitzgerald, our house master and wanted to surprise his old man. As soon as Mr Fitzgerald heard my voice outside, he recognised me by my voice immediately and said, 'Is that Jaidip?' He was really sharp and it was nearly thirty years since he had heard my voice last. I was really impressed by his memory.

One incident that comes to my mind involved our Hindi teacher at school, Mr Vimal, who was very short-tempered. One day, he slapped my friend Micky so hard in the face that Micky's spectacles went flying out of the classroom and fell in the garden below. Micky never cried or complained to his parents about this incident. Can you imagine this happening now? The teacher would have been suspended. Our lot were a tough bunch of boys and we knew, whatever the teachers were doing was good for us.

It was a boys' school and we were mild bullies too. A guy called Sudip Bose used to come every day with his mother's tiffin *shingara* and *gur sandesh*, and all that sort of stuff, and we would all ask, '*Ei ki enechish tiffin e ? Ma ke bolbi duto shingara diye dite*'. That is, what did you BRING today, tell your Mom to give two *samosas*, the Indian version of a closed taco or non-sweet pastry. We used to bully him but the fact is, one day we were greatly embarrassed. What happened was, it was his birthday and he invited us to his house. His father was present and suddenly, he told his dad, '*Baba baba erai amar khabar niye nay school e,*' these guys take my food in school. I think he went on to become a very good doctor.

One of my first memories of school was when I met Dada Osman, the well-known rugby (football with a oval ball) player; he was a senior in school and guided me through school at the beginning, later we became good friends.

THE PRINCIPAL, VICE-PRINCIPAL AND PREFECTS — 1959

STANDING: (L to R)—W. Sutton, V. Rao, A. Hussain, R. Nanda, I. Ahmed, S. Ghatak, J. Mukherjea, D. K. DE, A. Perry Keane.
SITTING: (L to R)—W. Banyard, S. Chatterjee, Mr. H. G. Chalke (The Principal), Mr. J. O. Vyse (Vice Principal), R. Mesrobian.

My best friend in school right through my school days was Dilip De (D K De). We were in the same class from the beginning till we passed out in December 1959.

D K and I were the best of buddies and knew everything about each other. He did really well in shipping; he opened his own company called Sealand, after leaving MacKinnon-McKenzie. We do not see each other very often now but keep tab on each other through D K's younger brother, Arjun De. Today D K lives in Mumbai, married to the author Shobha De. Calcutta's is a small society and everyone knows everyone, so we keep well informed about each other's welfare.

Another person who comes to my mind is my old friend Micky Chatterjee. He was the third person in our trio of Jaidip, Dilip and Micky. Unfortunately, Micky left school earlier and he did not finish with me and D K. We used to call him Pannu, he was a great person with a big heart.

A funny incident I recall with Micky was when I bunked school one day and went to Micky Chatterjee's house to fly kites. Micky was in school, so when I meet his mother, she was shocked to see me and asked me what I was doing in their house. I said that I had a day off, as I had to play a tennis match in the morning and asked her to give me Micky's kites, *manja* (the spice that is applied on the string to help cut the rival's kite) and *latai* (role of string). That whole afternoon I flew his kites till they were all destroyed and then I went home. I believe when Micky came home and found out that I had used up all his kites, he went berserk and he wouldn't talk to me for the next couple of weeks. I used to go to Micky's house very often, also for his mother's delicious mango pickles.

Dilip De

Micky Chatterjee

K P Singh Deo

Micky Chatterjee became one of my closest friends after school, and when I went to see him at the cancer hospital in his last days, the only person he recognised was me.

Another dear friend is the politician K P, who was very close to Micky and called him Micky Mouse. Micky used to campaign for K P during elections. D K, Micky, K P and I continued our friendship even after our school days; in fact, I am still in touch with D K and K P.

How can I forget K P Singh Deo, the Raja of Dhenkanal and former defense and information minister in the Government of India? K P and I were in the Hartley Kindergarten school and both of us joined La Martiniere together. K P's grandfather, the Raja of Keonjhar in Odisha and my grandfather, J C Mukerjea, were great friends and we took that friendship forward. K P now lives in Delhi and whenever I am in Delhi, I try to meet him or speak to him. He is a wonderful guy. K P Singh Deo is a great soul with a heart of gold and will do anything for his friends. He is a very good rower and represented India in rowing; he also became the president of the Indian Rowing Federation. When he was information minister in the Government of India, he helped the Indian Tennis Association a great deal by broadcasting live tennis tournaments around India. Other close friends from school were Romik Mesrobian, an Armenian boy who excelled in all sports and migrated to Australia. Former cricketer Shivaji Ray was in the same house (Martin House) and even now, whenever I meet him, he tells me I should have been a cricketer, as I was a very talented batsman.

When I was in school, I however, wanted to be a pilot and being a sports person was not really on my agenda though I was very good in all kinds of games. I considered games as a tool towards some other career. We had the National Cadet Corp (NCC) in school and I joined the air wing section. At first, I wanted to be a pilot because I used to look up to my uncle, Air Marshal Subroto Mukerjee, who became the first Indian to become an Air Marshal of the Indian Air Force (March 1911-November 1960). I hero-worshipped him and was very sad when he died in Tokyo when a chicken bone got stuck in his wind pipe during dinner in 1960. Those days, we were in a state of perpetual conflict with neighbours, Pakistan and China and some said, Air Marshal Mukerjee's death was an assassination that never got solved. One never knows the twists fate takes. My choice of tennis as a career was another such a twist.

Air Marshal Subroto Mukerjee

Chapter 3

THE TEMPLE OF TENNIS SOUTH CLUB

CALCUTTA'S FAMOUS SOUTH Club is where I started my career in tennis. South Club is now more than a hundred years old and that's where all the Davis Cup players from Calcutta began their tennis.

Calcutta was the place to be in, in the 1950s and '60s and the tournaments were part of the annual calendar for sports lovers in the country. Tennis tournaments in the South Club, Cricket test matches in Eden Gardens, Horse Racing and Polo at the Race Course, everyone from all over the country came to Calcutta for the winter because, apparently, it was the best place to be in. It was full of night clubs and good restaurants and had the famous 300 Club (which was before my time), it was a place where players could get breakfast at 6 am before they went to practice or went home after practice. Park Street was one of the places which was amazing. So, Calcutta was a swinging city in '50s and '60s and it is still now, but the ambience has changed.

CALCUTTA SOUTH CLUB LIMITED

Champions of India and Pride of South Club

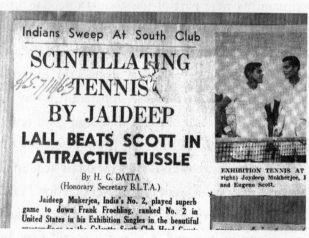

Indians Sweep At South Club

SCINTILLATING TENNIS BY JAIDEEP

LALL BEATS SCOTT IN ATTRACTIVE TUSSLE

By H. G. DATTA
(Honorary Secretary B.L.T.A.)

Jaideep Mukerjea, India's No. 2, played superb game to down Frank Froehling, ranked No. 2 in United States in his Exhibition Singles in the beautiful surroundings of the Calcutta South Club Hard Court.

EXHIBITION TENNIS AT right) Joydeep Mukherjee, I and Eugene Scott.

South Club was started in 1920 by three people, Anadi Mukherjee, Ganesh Dey and Akshay Dey. The story goes, one day, they were cycling down the road near the park and they saw some people playing tennis in another court. When the young men asked if they could play, they were told, sorry this club is not for Bengalis. This was the Punjab Club.

Very annoyed, Ganesh Dey and Akshay Dey went to my grandfather, J C Mukerjea. He was at that time the Chief Executive of the Calcutta Corporation and J M Sengupta (who was better known as Deshapriya) was the Mayor of the Corporation. Persistent, these three tennis enthusiasts finally got the land and the permission to build two courts where the club today lies, and that's how South Club came into being.

My memory of South Club goes back a very long time ago. I first went there at the age of seven or eight, 1950 or '51, with my grandfather, J C Mukerjea and father Adhip. My grandfather was one of the founding members of the club and was the president for many years. He was not only a BCCI president but also president of the Cricket Association of Bengal. He was, however, not a sports person as such but an administrator and a good sports manger. He always encouraged me and never stopped me from playing any games even during exam time.

I remember, Dadu used to have a lot of parties when he was president of the CAB. On the occasion of every cricket test match, he would have star players in the city, his Navy friends and important guests at the big dinner party he hosted for the two teams in the city. I used to hunt autographs of these important people and I wanted to be like them; I looked at these sportsmen and the fame that surrounded them. That is how I became glamour-struck.

My father was also the honorary secretary of the club for many years and always helped youngsters and encouraged them to play and be coached.

I USED TO go to the South Club often as a little boy to watch my father play tennis on the much-coveted lawns of the club. He was a good club player; he was a good all-round sportsman. The South Club has held many tournaments, it was the hub of tennis in India in the 1950s, '60s and '70s. The All-India Tennis Association was practically here in Calcutta at the South Club; the secretary was based in Calcutta.

All the tournaments that were hosted by the South Club were arranged by Ganesh Dey who was honorary secretary

The young tennis players who were being trained at the South Club under the Government of India coaching scheme initiated by the then Sports Minister Rajkumari Amrit Kaur.

at that time and his committee; and I remember it was really an annual ritual every winter to see the matches at the South Club. The South Club used to organise these tournaments and pay for the players to come all the way from Europe. Watching them play was a treat.

Dilip Bose

The reason why South Club produced so many tennis players was whenever our top players used to play, we had the opportunity to watch them play and see them practice. When I was very young, I used to watch Dilip Bose, Sumant Mishra and Naresh Kumar practice.

Sumant Mishra

Davis cup player Dilip Bose became a star coach.

Similarly, when Premjit, I and Akhtar were practicing in the South Club, youngster like Gaurav Misra, Bidyut Goswami, my younger brother Chirodeep, Narendar Singh, Praveen Singh, Nausher Madan, Rahul Basu and several others watched us.

Naresh Kumar

In those days, there were no television, no internet to watch top players play. The younger players would watch the seniors to get at least some idea of what the game was all about and they tried their best to follow.

I took to tennis accidentally, my father used to play at the South Club and they had started a coaching scheme which I had joined when I was nine years old. I soon left the class as I found it quite boring, when compared to other games like hockey, rugby and cricket. However, I had a freak car accident when I was ten and dislocated my left collar bone. That meant no rugby that summer.

So, my father once again dragged me to the South Club where, at that time, the Government of India had started a coaching scheme initiated by the then Sports Minister Rajkumari Amrit Kaur. Baba told me to play, and that's how my career in tennis started.

At the beginning, there were about fifty trainees and over the years, this increased to over 100. One of the trainees who joined the scheme was the most talented amongst us and was very handsome and he was none other than Premjit Lall who was the star pupil of the coaching scheme.

I started my tennis lessons under the formidable Dilip Bose, who had made his Davis Cup debut, way back in 1947. Under him all of us did very well. The urge to excel as a player and to represent my nation, emerged in me, from the very onset of my tennis training.

The coaching scheme was fantastic too. We had Dilip Bose as the chief coach who really took care of all the players. Dilip Bose saw the talent in Premjit and me and worked more and more with us. Panchu Gopal Singh was another great guy who played regularly with me every afternoon.

Then we had a couple of foreign coaches who came to Kolkata, like we had Hans Nüsslein from Germany who was a legend in the International Tennis Hall of Fame.

There was also a Mr Lawrence from the UK, who was here for the Rajkumari Amrit Kaur coaching scheme. He used to work with me and Premjit, so we were lucky to have a foreign coach.

Sydney Mathews was in charge of the morning coaching scheme. He was a very good player; though a base liner, he dedicated his life to morning coaching and used to train us early in the morning. This morning coaching session is still going on at the South Club. This is the 'pay and play' scheme and Mathew did a fantastic job. Unfortunately, he died quite young from cancer of the throat.

South Club is the only club in India which encourages pay and play – that is, basically anyone can play tennis in the club; this is one of the reasons why the land was given to the club.

When I began playing, our first lesson used to be at 7 am, before school. After us came the wives of important city officials, senior policemen and sons of diplomats in the city. All the courts were in use in the morning with people queuing up to play, have breakfast and go to work by ten. We returned after school to play for a while and then the adults played under floodlights, late into the night.

Premjit had fantastic strokes, good looks and all the girls swooned over him and all the boys including myself were very jealous of him; Premjit was a year-and-a-half older and had a game to be a top-class tennis player which he became; his only flaw was that he was not really quick around the court and had a short temper which went against him. He also did not play that well under pressure.

I was the second-best player but was way behind Premjit; but I was a natural athlete and a fighter and played well under pressure and this helped me to win some big matches. In the early days, Premjit used to beat me easily, in fact I think I lost to him more than ten times in our junior days, this frustrated me and made me work harder and finally, I beat him in the Calcutta Hard Court Championship at South Club in 1958.

Though rivals in tennis, Premjit and I were great friends and continued to be so until his dying day.

Dilip Bose was a strict disciplinarian and took no nonsense from his trainees. It is because of him that Premjit and I became top class tennis players. I remember, I had a natural sliced backhand which was pretty good. Dilip Bose changed it and made me hit top spin backhand, which eventually I mastered. The reason Dilip changed my backhand was that he also had a sliced backhand and later, when he played against top-class players of his time, he could not pass them in the net as he did not have a top spin back hand. He did not want that to happen to me. To this day, I thank him for changing my back hand.

I consider Dilip Bose as one of the best coaches India has produced, because he had an eye for talent and picked them up and worked with them. God knows how many times he hit me with his tennis racquet on my calf, just to bend my knees, this is part of coaching. To be able to produce top class tennis players is not a joke and he did that with Premjit and me. I am really grateful to him because, had Dilip Bose not been around, I don't think I would have become a tennis player.

When the coaching scheme started in real earnest, I was straight away put in the advance group that comprised Premjit Lall, P Kohli, Tutu Bose, P Chopra and a few others. We received individual coaching from Dilip Bose and he was a very tough task master.

We also had the special coaching in the morning at 7 am before going to school. My day would start very early, at 6 am and I would cycle to South Club from Alipore to play tennis, then go to school till 1 pm. I had my lunch at my grandmother's house which was close to the South Club and rushed back to South Club at around 2 pm for further coaching. Then I went back to school at about 4 pm to play hockey, cricket or rugby, depending on the time of the year and then cycle back all the way to Alipore. By the time I did my homework and went to bed, I was very exhausted. In fact, this schedule helped me to be fitter and stronger.

I started playing tournaments from the age of eleven in the local junior tournaments and the Men's events. The special coaching, drills and workouts that Dilip Bose gave us from

2 to 3.30 pm, no matter how hot it was, made us really tough. By the time I was 16 years old, there were only three of us left in the group – Premjit, Paramjit Kohli and I. Kohli stopped playing after he finished the junior year and joined a corporate house. So, it was only Premjit and I from the old South Club scheme who kept the national flag flying.

WHILE PREMJIT AND I were training under Dilip Bose at South Club, Akhtar Ali, who was a bit older than me, was making waves in Indian tennis. Akhtar started tennis under the guidance of his father Asgar Ali, a tennis and squash coach of Saturday Club. Akhtar was slightly short but had loads of talent. He was the national junior champion and also reached the junior Wimbledon semi-final in 1957. Akhtar was also a very fine squash player and won the national squash singles tournament.

In 1955, the then Maharani of Jaipur, Ayesha Devi who was a keen tennis player, recognised Akhtar's talent and started sponsoring him as Akhtar came from very humble roots. The Maharani sent Akhtar for special coaching to England and that's how his career blossomed.

Akhtar also played at Wimbledon and other international tournaments but is better known as one of India's best tennis coaches. He was the coach of the Indian Davis Cup team from 1966 to 1996, and has coached a lot of top Indian players such as Vijay Amritraj, Ramesh Krishnan and many others.

He was also in charge of the South Club coaching scheme for many years and has produced Davis Cup players such as Gaurav Misra, Chirodeep Mukerjea, Bidyut Goswami, Narendar Singh, Shyam Minotra, S Fazaluddin, not to mention Leander Paes.

Apart from these players, Akhtar also produced players who made a mark in international tennis such as Enrico Piperno, Nausher Madan, Praveen Singh and the talented Dilip Kumar, who at the time of writing has just passed away. Rahul Basu and others started playing under coach Akhtar Ali after he retired from competitive tennis and became the National Coach of India. He also coached his son Zeeshan Ali, who is at present India's Davis Cup coach and has himself won six National Singles titles and played Davis Cup for India.

Akhtar was a very jovial person, with lots of jokes in his repertoire. He also sang well and entertained the teams in the circuit. In earlier days, he, being the senior, used to guide me through the circuit. We had some very good double wins together and beat Newcombe and Fletcher from Australia and Manuel Santana and José Arilla from Spain in the international tournament at Istanbul. It was unfortunate that the South Club did not renew Akhtar's coaching contract. I was not in the committee at that time, otherwise this would not have happened.

A view of South Club lawns.

NO OTHER CLUB in the country can perhaps match the contribution of Kolkata's South Club to tennis in India.

The Club used to regularly organise tournaments similar to the Wimbledon, and from day one, the stadiums used to be full, with three to four thousand people watching at a time, from the early rounds itself. The finals were between the top players like Swen Davidsson of Sweden, Jaroslav Drobny, World no.1 Roy Emerson, Bob Hewitt, Martin Mulligan, Fred Stolle – they all played in the South Club tournaments in India. South Club used to invite them, pay for their fare and after playing at South Club, they would go around the country, playing elsewhere.

We had a very good tennis circuit in Kolkata at the time. In the summer we started with the Ordinance Club tournament, followed by the Cossipur Club tournament and then the Calcutta Hard Court which was held in South Club in September just before Durga Puja. In January, we had the Calcutta Gym Khana tournament followed by the Shyambazaar Club tournament and then the CC&FC tournament. In addition, we had the Saturday Club tennis tournament which was started by Premjit, I and Akhtar Ali and is still the most popular tennis tournament in Kolkata.

South Club has produced many Davis Cup players – Sumant Misra, Dilip Bose, Naresh Kumar, Premjit Lall, Akhtar Ali,

Jaidip Mukerjea, going down all the way to Leander, Zeeshan Ali, Fazaluddin and several others. Naresh Kumar, our Davis Cup captain at that time, was looking after his family's coal business and was a very good friend of Russi Mody; in fact, thanks to Russi, his business blossomed and soon he became one of the biggest coal merchants in India. Naresh did an excellent job of expanding his company and today, his son Arjun looks after the business, though Naresh even at the age of 90 years, went to the office regularly. He passed away at the ripe age of 92 on 14 September 2022.

Ajit Lall, Premjit's brother and Anwar Ali, Akhtar's brother were good tennis players. Ajit represented India in junior tournaments. There were also Shyam Minotra and Vinay Dhavan, all great players; unfortunately, Shyam and Vinay died quite young but they played for India in the Asian Games, Shyam had also played for the Davis Cup.

Other players have also done very well; some of them have very good coaching jobs in USA. Today they all reminisce about South Club and are nostalgic about our evening after-game chats at a place which was a home, away from home for all of us. We talk of the fun we used to have, playing cricket in the clay courts during the cricket season, with tennis ball cricket which was very popular.

Calcutta was vivacious in the 1960s and we had a South Club gang. We used to go to the movies for the 9 o' clock show; it was fashionable to go to the movies in halls like Light House, Metro and Elite where after the night show was over, a band used to play, we used to sing and dance to music. There

Our Park Street gang in the mid-60s; from left Dilip De, Bonny Kent, Gopal Rana, Rahul Dasgupta, Jaidip Mukerjea and Mahesh Malhotra, taken in Trincas.

was a bar in a miniature hall where impromptu parties would happen; we were very friendly with Khem Shamsher (the owner of halls like Lighthouse and New Empire), so it was good fun. We would hang out in CCFC or the Saturday Club and then in Park Street. There were night clubs like Firpos, Princess, Trincas and several others. At that time, anyone who mattered in society came to Kolkata to enjoy Christmas.

Little did we know that history was soon to serve Calcutta a raw deal, a war with China in the winter of 1962, which we allegedly lost. As a result, the 20,000 ethnic Chinese in the city (mostly in Tiretta Bazaar area, Tangra) began to be looked at as aliens; the restaurant scene changed when more than 3,000 people of Chinese origin were interned in security camps.

The BBC reported in January 1964, 'More than 100 people have been killed following Hindu-Muslim rioting in the Indian city of Calcutta' and 'Over 7,000 people have also been arrested and 438 injured in the clashes which have spread to the surrounding districts'. There was anti-Hindu atrocities in neighbouring East Bengal too. India's terms with the western neighbour, Pakistan was no good. The Reserve Bank of India kept devaluing the rupee from 1963 to 1967, as a result, the local economy suffered. The city was clearly on the edge.

By the early sixties, I had carved out my name in the international tennis circuits, at Wimbledon and Davis Cup, and felt proud to be a city boy. I was also representing my country. If I was not travelling, I was an invitee at all the big parties. I was flamboyant and loved at all the sports clubs and was visible at the races and cricket matches and polo matches, gala events and night clubs. I was buoyant, winning some, losing some. It was in these tempestuous times that I married Brenda Lilley, the singer.

On hindsight, I think I married too young, I was just about 22, with a blossoming sports career ahead and hectic travel throughout the year. Our lifestyles were, obviously, not compatible. We have three daughters, Shalini, Malini and Anisa. After our divorce in the 1990s, I looked after the girls and educated them to the best of my ability. Shalini went to London and my other two daughters went to colleges in the USA. They are all grown up now, married and have their own children.

To return to the sixties and seventies, a lot of my friends who came to the clubs and joined our *adda*, became Naxals. Subhash Ganguly ran away after an arrest warrant against him. Students of the Presidency, St Xaviers and St Stephens, all wanted to be revolutionaries. And many of them had associations with the South Club, as a sports hotspot. After that, during the CPIM rule, most club staff were unionised; they removed the English language from the curriculum and did away with most British traditions in Calcutta's cultural life.

Calcutta's Club culture was great in the '60 and '70s. When I first joined the South Club officially as a member in 1965, I was already a member of Saturday Club, and then the Tolly Club which served excellent British food. I used to have Mulligatawny soup for lunch, grilled fish, sausages with mash, a steak or a steak in kidney pie and caramel custard; these were a staple. Indian food too was there. The British did not encourage tipping of the staff; nor was there a donation like there is today in the Bengal Club and Calcutta Club. In Saturday Club, the bearers have kept up the tradition.

South Club even in the '70s and '80s used to be the place to be in. Among the notable members of the clubs were Manish Sabharwal, managing director of Dunlop, Keshub Mahindra, chairman of the Mahindra group who is now a hundred years old and was a very good tennis player; in fact, if he had continued, he could have played for India at that time. There were also C E Cargin of Jessop and Co, Sir Walter Michel More, the chief of Bird and Co, and a host of other Englishmen who were all very good tennis players and played at the South Club. Then there were others like John Withnell and Frank Thompson who I saw playing at the South Club. Among players just below the top standards were Ivan Alexy and Eddy Abrecht who were the main distributors in India for Omega watches at that time.

Old man Sir L P Misra was my grandfather's age and was

one of the old doyens of the club and helped the club all the time in different ways. He was the chief of Hindustan Motors when it was set up and we had a lot of support from him. I still remember him coming to South Club and giving us lectures on how to play, how to behave etc. He was a great source of inspiration for Premjit, me and all the young players. His son Sumant Misra and grandson, both, were national champions and represented the country in the Davis Cup.

I first met the film star Amitabh Bachchan in 1963, when he came to Kolkata looking for a job; Calcutta those days was where the action was and people from all over the country came to Calcutta for jobs. At that time, we did not know what his future held – that one-day Amitabh would be a superstar.

He used to share a room with our common friends at the boarding house called Clacton's on Russell Street, which is off Park Street, the most happening street in Kolkata in those days.

He first joined Bird & Co and then went on to join a freight-booking company called Blacker. He was a keen sportsman and played some tennis with me at the famous South Club. Amitabh was a real charmer with the opposite sex, with his lanky frame and dark and handsome looks, but he was also a very humble man. Those days, Amit and I used to spend a lot of time together and used to go to the same parties. We had some great times together.

However, his first love was acting and soon he joined a theatre group called Amateurs who did English plays in and around Kolkata. We called him Amit. Amit's aim was to go to Mumbai and succeed there and that he did and how!!

Amit was a very shy person but when he opened up, he really opened up – with his baritone voice. He used to play the dholak and sing and be very friendly with Gopal Banerjee, another member of the South Club. Gopal's brother Prabhat Banerjee is a member of the South Club. Whenever I see him on television now, I marvel at how Amit has kept himself so well all these years, and admire him for what he has done for our country, God bless him. We haven't met for ages and I hope we can meet sometime soon to talk about our early years. It was my pleasure knowing him from close quarters.

The first secretary of the club was Anadi Mukherjee, he was a very good administrator and he was helped by assistant secretary Ganesh Dey. After the demise of Anadi Mukherjee, Ganesh Dey became the secretary. He is the one responsible for the beautiful grass courts we have in Calcutta, which as I said earlier, compare with the best grass courts of the world including Wimbledon.

Dey knew every part of the land and even when he was old, he came to the South Club every day and he truly was an institution in tennis circles in India. He worked for H Wheeler & Co who were agents for Slazenger in India and Mr Dey gave Premjit, me and Akhtar free racquets to play; we were all very thankful to Ganesh Dey for giving us such a beautiful club.

SOUTH CLUB IS paradise for tennis players in India, with twelve grass courts and six clay courts. When I became South Club president for the second time, I thought to change the surfaces, so now we have six red clay courts, five hard courts and six grass courts and a beautiful swimming pool for members to enjoy.

When we joined the Rajkumari Amrit Kaur coaching scheme, our dressing room was behind the club office, we were not allowed to use the main dressing room then. We had to come from the back of the office rooms, go to our (the trainee) changing room, change and go to the tennis court, change and then go out. Unless one was invited to go to the club dressing room, one could not do so.

All this has changed – not for the better but for the worse and I think our past presidents must all be turning in their graves to see where the club has gone in this respect.

There are two outsourced restaurants now. The bar used to be our *adda* spot. It was great for us; after playing tennis for a while all of us, including sportsmen from other games, went to the bar and had a drink and reminisced about the old times in tennis, football and cricket. It was great fun to be gathering in the bar after matches. Alas, nowadays the bar is empty and when one goes there these days, there is no sportsman in the bar, no one to talk to about cricket, football or tennis. The bar remains the same but work is on for an extension behind the clay courts, where players and members can come from elsewhere and enjoy the facilities of the club.

Once upon a time, the food in South Club was simply amazing – breakfast in the morning, the scrambled eggs, toast and omelette were actually fantastic; the fresh lime soda of the Calcutta South Club used to be deemed the best in Kolkata; and during international tournaments, the famous dish of chicken curry and rice was popular with everyone, including the players and foreign players; but the taste of South Club you could not resist was the chicken cutlet which was fabulous for all. Everyone from all over India and Calcutta came to South Club to enjoy the food, which was simple, tasty and healthy.

We also had some very honest and caring Bearers – in the kitchen we had Bilayat Khan and Shanti Lal, the two of them were in charge of the small kitchen and the bar. In the dressing room, we had our Head Bearer Banshi; then we had Bhagawan Das, Kalindi and Benu. Kalindi's son Sridhar is today South Club's Head Bearer. Benu's son Bijay Das was for years South Club's accountant and has now retired. They were the second generation employees of the club. The club encouraged all the ball boys to be coaches and encouraged them to play free tennis and some of the ball boys at my time are today tennis coaches all over India and doing really well.

Banshi, the Head dressing room Bearer, kept a scrap book of all the players who had trained at the club, with all the clippings of the players. Every morning he would read all the newspapers and collect the tennis cuttings and he would then paste them in the scrap book. There were around six to seven large scrapbooks of yore, courtesy Banshi Bearer. Whenever I, Premjit and Akhtar came back after our long tours of Europe and the States, we would go for the scrap book and see if our names were there. Our names were always there, Banshi made it a habit of keeping everyone there, he did not know how to speak English properly but he knew how to read and write. Full credit to Banshi for his love for South Club and for tennis. The scrap books are lost now for some reason. It would have been an utterly amazing archival record for today's youngsters to go through the newspaper cuttings of old matches, had these scrapbooks been preserved.

The club now has an air-conditioned dressing room, which we old-time players feel is not needed; not good for players to move to court and from court to AC conditions. I remember the old days when Premjit, I and Akhtar Ali used to practice and then go out to have breakfast and go home to get ready for school. We used to come back in the early afternoon, say after school, around one thirty-two and sleep in the dressing room, rest for a while in the dressing room rather, on the rexine sofas and the fans would whirl slowly as we tried to rest. Then we got to the tennis courts after half an hour or so to start our practice sessions.

SOUTH CLUB ALSO had other sportsmen playing tennis – stars like Chuni Goswami, Shyam Thapa, Laltu Bhattacharya, Pradip Choudhury and several others. There were a few senior IPS officers who would come to the club regularly; there was Biren Saha, a former Police commissioner; Tushar Talukdar, also a former police commissioner who became the president of South Club. The practice started with P K Sen and B K Saha, and senior police officers still continue to play

Chuni Goswami

tennis at the South Club. Others like Raj Kanojia, Harmenpreet Singh, S N Gupta, Johore are still members and come to play tennis regularly.

In the 1980s, the South Club had a football team, led by Chuni Goswami and South Club used to play matches with some other football teams in Kolkata. Chuni was still very good and even at that time, his dribbling was fantastic and great to watch.

It is in the South Club that I got friendly with the former Indian football Captain, Chuni Goswami who was an international sportsman and won the football gold medal in the Asian Games in 1962. He was the Captain of the Bengal cricket team that went to the Ranji Trophy finals. Chuni started playing tennis at the South Club rather late but had a good game. I played with him in a couple of tournaments and we won these tournaments in Kolkata. His elder brother, Manik Goswami, was also a close friend of mine. He later became an important office-bearer of the Bengal Tennis Association. I have great memories of them and I have had some great times with Chuni and Manik. I travelled with Mani to Wimbledon and Chuni came with me when we opened the tennis academy in Siliguri.

Chuni and I met each other every day at the South Club, which, after all was a sports club. Chuni passed away in 2020. His son plays golf for the Royal Calcutta Golf Club.

Another football legend who I was friends with was P K Banerjee, he and Chuni were the greatest Bengali football

P K Banerjee

players ever produced. PK was a great human being, though we didn't play tennis together, he watched all the club matches and knew all the tennis statistics of various players. He was also an amazing football coach who took the clubs East Bengal and Mohun Bagan to the highest level of national football.

Notu Roy of Philips organised the football matches which were sponsored by Philips, and he was a very nice person. I remember P B Dutt (Badalda), the former captain of Bengal's Ranji Trophy team, my old friend Micky Chatterjee and Laltu Bhattacharya, who even now is a regular fixture at the club bar. My good friend Alok Pratap Sen used to grace our adda regularly along with Shyam Thapa and Pradip Choudhury, as did two other very good tennis players who played regularly with us, the two brothers Somenath Bose and Satinath Bose. Vace Paes, Leander's father, and a few others also played at the South Club.

I became a club committee member at a very young age and I have held all the post in Calcutta's South Club, starting with committee Member and going up the seniority ladder to assistant secretary and secretary for many years. Then I was chosen to be the president of the best sports club in Asia. I was the third generation of the Mukerjeas to play at the club.

The club was called the Wimbledon of the East and we had the best grass courts, east of the Suez Canal those days. I think it to be as good as Wimbledon because several players on the grass court from South Club Kolkata did well at Wimbledon.

Centenary Celebrations of Calcutta South Club

2020 WAS THE centenary year of South Club, and as luck would have it, I was the president at that time.

We had two wonderful functions, the first was to felicitate Dr Abhijit Banerjee who won the Nobel Prize for Economics in 2019.

Banerjee is an avid tennis player and plays regularly; he learnt his tennis at a South Club coaching scheme under Akhtar Ali. We are honoured that he has become a fellow member of our club. The second function was to felicitate top-ranking and Davis Cup players who have played and won tournaments on

At the South Club celebrations with Leander Paes and Anil Mukherji, CEO Tollygunge Club (next to Jaidip).

our beautiful grass courts which compare favourably with the grass courts of Wimbledon.

Leading the brigade was none other than the Tennis maestro Ramanathan Krishnan who I consider the best player India has produced; among those who attended the gala function were Anand Amritraj, Ramesh Krishnan, Mahesh Bhupathi, Jasjit Singh and club members who did us proud like Akhtar

Ali, Zeeshan Ali and others. It was a lovely fun-filled evening, though very nostalgic as we all met after a long time.

We at the club had planned a lot of events for 2020 but unfortunately, due to the pandemic everything was cancelled or postponed. Such is life.

Chapter 4

GRADUATING TO WIMBELDON

I DID WELL in the local tournaments when I was in school and used to win most of the junior titles and used to get to the semifinals and finals of the Men's events. Thus, I became the National Junior Champion under 13 in 1955 and the Under 18 Champion in 1958-59. After this, I stopped playing the junior tournament and concentrated on the Senior events.

Playing the Indian circuit at that time were S P Misra, Ajit Kumar (who later became the Finance Secretary to the Government of India), Vinay Dhawan, Gopal Banerjee and Shyam Minotra. Among them, S P Misra and Shyam Minotra represented India in the Davis Cup and Vinay Dhawan represented India in the Asian games.

After I finished school in December 1959, I played all the tournaments in the circuit and every summer used to go to Europe, first to the UK to play tournaments like Surbiton, Manchester, Bristol and Beckenham and the big one at Wimbledon.

A PASSIONATE
AFFAIR

Wimbledon *HS 23. 6/70*

Laver makes a confident start

Lal and Mukherjea move up

From SYDNEY FRISKIN

LONDON, JUNE 22.—The Wimbledon Lawn Tennis Championships which opened here today in bright sunshine had no surprises although it is feared that its tranquillity might yet be disturbed by demonstration against some of the South African players.

Ramanathan Krishnan looks on as Jaideep Mukerjea volleys a winner during their Junior win in the doubles match of the Austriala India 1966 Cup tie at Kooyong, Melbourne.

DAVIS CUP 39

After Wimbledon, most of the top players played in Europe as the appearance money in Europe was far better than in the USA and they hosted the players. So only some of the players went to the USA.

When I first went to England before Wimbledon, to play other tournaments, I made it a point to go to Wimbledon and see the Centre Court and the other courts and get a feel of the atmosphere. Before I went to Wimbledon, we used to follow Wimbledon on radio (BBC) and I used to get really worked up by the commentary by the famous commentator of those days, Dan Maskell, and I would imagine playing on the Centre Court at Wimbledon. These experiences really made me work harder, because by that time I was determine to play in the Wimbledon.

In 1959, after I had played in England for a month or so,

began the Qualifying Round for Wimbledon which I managed to get into. Luckily for me, I qualified in my first attempt and never had to do that again. I won 3 rounds but it was nerve-racking when you don't know who you are going to play with, what type of players they are; nevertheless, I managed to win the Qualifier.

In the first round that year, I lost to the Polish number 1, Wladyslaw Skonecki. This was really an exciting time for me, because finally a part of my dream was beginning to come true – that I had participated in Wimbledon. In 1959, when I was selected to represent India at the Junior Wimbledon, I reached the semi-finals and had to give a walkover in the Semis, as I had sprained my ankle very badly.

In 1959, I also qualified for the Main draw for the Men's Singles event at the Wimbledon and was really happy, as now I would be matching swords with the big guns in tennis.

Then, in 1960 again I reached the Wimbledon Junior finals and lost in three close sets to a South African player named

Wladyslaw Skonecki

Rodney Mandelstam. I regret this to this day as I was leading all the way but sadly, on that day I could not win. This was one of my major disappointments.

This was really my start in international tennis. Wimbledon was the Holy Grail of tennis and every player wanted to win at Wimbledon or at least be part of this tournament. Fortunately for me, I played Wimbledon for sixteen successive years from 1959 to 1974.

The first year when I went to Wimbledon, I took a 4-hour flight to Bombay from Kolkata. Then I took an Air India super constellation plane from Bombay to London, via Beirut and Rome. I remember when I was sitting on the London bound flight, I saw the engine start and a lot of fire come out of the engine. I quickly unfastened my seatbelt and was about to leave my seat, but to my pleasant surprise I saw the airhostess smiling and serving. When I told her about the fire she only laughed and told me, there was nothing to worry about, when the engine starts sparks fly. I was really terrified, but she put me at ease.

My record at Wimbledon has been exceptional when compared to Indian standards. I reached the last 16, four times – in 1963, 1964, 1966 and 1973.

In 1963 I lost to winner Chuck McKinley in the Centre Court; I was really nervous to play in the Centre Court; that was one of my ambitions which came true. In 1964, I lost to Bob Hewitt in Court number 2; he had just played a great match that day and I thought I had a chance of winning as he would be tired, but he just beat me in straight sets.

Chuck McKinley

Ken Fletcher

Bob Hewitt

In 1966, I lost in the last 16 to my good friend, Australia's Ken Fletcher. I don't know how I lost that match I was winning. It was played in court number 1 on a Saturday afternoon. I won the first set 6-2, I lead 5-2 on the second set and I had 2 sets point in his serve. I saw a black cloud coming in and it was gonna rain, I was serving 5-3 to win the second set and seeing the dark clouds overhead, I hurried and doing so, I lost my serve. Then there was a break and it poured. We waited for two hours. Finally, when we returned to court, he won the second set 9-7. And he won the third set 6-4 and then there was more rain again and the play was stopped for the day. Anyway, my concentration was lost.

We came back on Monday because Sunday was a rest day and started the match with Fletcher leading me to 2 sets to 1.

I won the 4th set and finally lost the fifth 6-1. This was a great disappointment because I could have reached the Quarter-final and become the second Indian to get to the Quarter-final before Ramanathan Krishnan. Krishnan reached the Semi-finals twice.

In 1973, in open Wimbledon I lost to young Jan Kodeš in 4 sets. It was a pretty close match, Kodeš went on to win Wimbledon and so, it was a very satisfying tournament for me.

We did great in the Doubles and we reached the doubles Quarter-finals thrice, twice with Premjit Lall and once with Ramanathan Krishnan.

Even now, I make it a point to be at Wimbledon during the tournament as often as I can because there we get to meet a lot of friends and colleagues, who still come to play or come to watch – player like Roger Taylor, a very good friend of mine, Tony Roche, Thomas Koch, and an American like Charlie Pasarell, who owns one of the biggest tournaments in the world, the Indian Wells, California. So, it's a place to be and I always prefer Wimbledon to other Grand Slams because it is the ultimate for us Indians.

Jan Kodeš   **Roger Taylor**   **Thomas Koch**   **Charlie Pasarell**

Chapter 5

———◆———

BAPTISM BY FIRE
THE DAVIS CUP

MY MUCH-CHERISHED DREAM, to represent my country, finally became a reality in 1960.

It was in the month of April and I was in Lahore, playing the Pakistan National Championship. When much to my pleasant surprise, a telegram arrived from the All-India Tennis Association asking me to reach Bangkok at the earliest and join the Indian Davis Cup squad, for their tie against Thailand.

Abandoning my plans to play another tournament in Karachi, I rushed back to Kolkata, only to catch a flight for Bangkok. I arrived in Bangkok at around 4 pm, on my eighteenth birthday, 21 April 1960.

Upon reaching the hotel in which the Indian Team of Ramanathan Krishnan and Naresh Kumar were put up (modest in comparison today), I was shocked to find that our senior member, Ramanathan Krishnan, was down with chicken pox.

Thus, the Indian Team for the tie now comprised Naresh Kumar and Jaidip, both from the same club (Calcutta South Club) and city (Kolkata), playing in the 49th edition of the Davis Cup.

On 22 April, at 11 am, just about eighteen hours after I landed at the venue city, with no practice on the venue courts, I was pitted to play the first Singles match of the day. My opponent was Sutiraphan Karalak. Though the situation was somewhat daunting for an eighteen-year-old, I decided to give it my all, in order to do justice to the opportunity that I had been bestowed.

Gathering all my wits together, I started the match, winning the first set in a nail-bitter. The match eventually stretched to five sets, and proved quite a thriller for the home crowd. Finally, in the fifth set, I managed the last laugh with a see-saw score line of 11-9, 0-6, 6-2,3-6, & 6-3.

The win proved to be a great morale booster for my journey in Davis Cup. Later in the day, Naresh Kumar played some great tennis to demolish Seri Charuchinda in straight sets, to give India a 2-0 lead on that first day.

But, it was on the second day, when Naresh and I beat the Thai pair Karalak and Sudasana, to clinch the tie for the nation, that great wonder struck me. I was on Cloud Nine. Even today, I cannot explain the emotion which ran through this eighteen-year-old kid, debuting for his nation and being instrumental in his country's victory.

THOUGH I BECAME a regular member of Indian Davis Cup squad from 1960 onwards, the most memorable year in Davis Cup for me shall always be 1966. It was the year in which, the squad reached the Finals for the Challenge Round, as it was known as till 1971.

The year had started on a great note. The team comprising Ramanathan Krishnan (as Captain), Premjit Lall, S P Misra and I trounced Iran in Ahmedabad and Sri Lanka (then Ceylon) in Trivandrum (now Thiruvananthapuram) convincingly, to set up the East Zone title clash with Japan.

The Japan-India tie was held in Tokyo from 30 September, where we managed to pull off a convincing 4-1 victory against the host nation.

Thus, from Tokyo, our road led to the famous green lawns

of the Delhi Gymkhana for the Inter-Zonal Semi-final tie, to be played between India (the Asian Zone Champion) and West Germany (the European Zone Champion). Since I had won the National Tennis Championship on the same lawns earlier that year, beating Premjit, the choice of the venue gave me an added confidence for the upcoming tie.

The squad reached Delhi in the first week of November. The organisers of the tie had thankfully arranged our stay at Claridges, a hotel close to the venue, and provided us the much-needed comfort required after the gruelling practice sessions. The weather in Delhi and the ambience at Delhi Gymkhana was just perfect for us to take on then West Germany. For the tie, the German team comprised the much-fancied Wilhelm Bungert and Ingo Buding. The team was coached by none other than Kurt Nielson, who held the distinction of being the first Dane to reach the Wimbledon Finals.

Wilhelm Bungert and Ingo Buding

Kurt Nielson

The tie started on 12 November. To our surprise, the stands were completely filled. People of varied ages and from various walks of life had thronged the stands with the expectation to witness some great tennis.

Krishnan and I did not disappoint the crowd on the first day. An inspired Krishnan defeated Wilhelm Bungert in straight sets. Many thought this to be an upset, considering the form Bungert was in and his record that year. In the next match, I managed a win against Ingo Buding in four sets. We, thus, gave India a 2-0 lead over our rivals. The two wins lit the fire of a possible India win, on the very first day.

Next day disappointment struck us from the very early morning. Krishnan woke up with a stiff back and we had to change the previously decided doubles combination of Premjit and Krishnan. I was asked to step in and partner Premjit, to play the German duo of Bungert and Buding. Even though we

put up a decent show, stretching the second set into a score line of 8-10, the German pair eventually got the better of us and kept themselves in contention for the tie.

The Final Day being a Sunday generated a huge gathering at the temporarily constructed stands. Many distinguished guests were also present, including the legendary actor Dilip Kumar along with his newly-wed bride, the very gorgeous Saira Banu. It seemed, to disappoint such a high-spirited crowd would amount to indulging in a sinful act. On the other hand, Bungert, after his loss to Krishnan, was raring to go at me in the first reverse Singles match. Little was he aware that I was also determined to prove my mettle.

Maybe the pressure of the situation got a little better of me in the beginning. I lost the first set rather tamely at 6-4. But, in the following three sets, I decided not to give anything away without a bitter fight to the end. Thus, after the end of the fourth set, the final score line read 4-6, 8-6, 8-6, 6-3, in favour of Jaidip Mukerjea.

I can still remember the ecstasy of the crowd, as India emerged victorious in the tie and took another step forward in its quest to challenge the mighty Australians at Melbourne for the Challenge Round. We were now pitted to play against Brazil in our next tie, in order to book our tickets for Melbourne.

Chapter 6

JOYOUS KOLKATA, CHEERING MELBOURNE

AFTER OUR EMPHATIC win against West Germany, we were now scheduled to meet the giant-killer Brazil, for the Semi-final tie. I call the Brazilian team as giant-killers, as they had overcome the formidable US team, which comprised stalwarts like Arthur Ashe and Dennis Ralston, to reach the Semi-final round.

So, when after an intense round of consultations with the senior-most member of the Indian Team, Ramanathan Krishnan and many others, the All-India Tennis Association announced the coveted grass courts of the Calcutta South Club as the venue of the Semi-final, I was extremely thrilled, as it would give me the opportunity to perform in front of my father (who was also the secretary of the club at that time), my mentor Dilip Bose and others, all who I have had a profound influence on my career.

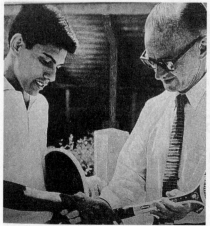

NO... it's not the Davis Cup. But, above, Indian tennis team members Ramanathan Krishnan (left); captain Raj Khanna and Jaideep Mukerjea are no doubt hoping that they'll be able to repeat this pose tonight, holding the real thing.

As I was present in the city during the preparation of the tie, I can tell you that setting up an arrangement to accommodate about 5,000 spectators and to arrange for all that was required to host a tie of this stature was quite a challenging task for the officials. Rising to the occasion, members of the club like Naresh Kumar, Ganesh Dey, Subroto Bose, Adhip Mukerjea, Dilip Bose and many others, worked round the clock, to make it a grand success. The hospitality extended to both the teams and guests was extremely warm and the club and the courts lived up to their reputation as the Wimbledon of the East.

Though Premjit and I were sweating it out for the tie from the time we reached Kolkata from Delhi, we were joined by Krishnan and Misra just about a week before the tie, which was to start from 4 December 1966. Another luminous Kolkata boy, my friend Akthar Ali, was also with us as the coach of the team along with an AITA official and our non-playing captain, Shamser Singh.

The center court for the tie was prepared at the very place where the synthetic court No.2 lies today. After a few practice sessions, the Indian Team members were quite satisfied with the surface. It was pretty fast and even, and we all thought that would definitely give some advantage to the host team, as the team comprised players who had considerable success on such courts.

Soon the Brazilian Team arrived, to dampen our spirits to some extent, we found that Thomaz Koch and José Edison Mandarino were in great form and in high spirits and were determined to repeat their success story against the USA, in the Quarter-finals.

In the very first match of the tie, I was pitted against the blazing Thomaz Koch, who happened to outplay me in straight sets, to take the lead for Brazil.

In the second match, which was between our top-seed Krishnan and José Mandarino, it seemed Mandarino was eager to repeat his giant-killing feat against Dennis Ralston. Unfortunately, this time he was against a might called Ramanathan Krishan, who, after having lost the first set, very calmly changed the pace of the game to eventually alter the fate of the match and tie. The score line at the end read- 5-7,6-2,6-2,6-3, in favour of Krishnan, much to our relief and to the relief of nearly 5,000 spectators, including many who were on tree-tops and terraces of nearby high-rises – many of which were still under construction – eager to witness history unfolding.

On the second day, a little unfortunate incident took place in the dressing room before the crucial doubles match. Our coach and Krishnan decided to field me for the doubles match, instead of Premjit Lall, after witnessing the form and style of the Brazilian Team. The news dealt a bit of a blow to my friend Premjit, as he too was eager to play in front of his home crowd. Just after a few minutes though, when Krishnan and I took the field to face the challenge of Koch-Mandarino, Premjit's cheer was perhaps the loudest. Such was our camaraderie, which I cherish, even today.

The doubles match turned out to be extremely entertaining, with tables turning constantly in favour of and against both the teams. Finally, the score read, 7-5, 3-6, 6-3, 3-6, 6-3, resembling more like a game of Snakes & Ladders than Tennis, in favour of us and giving India the crucial 2-1 lead in the tie. The voice of Krishnan from that match still echoes in my mind, asking me to attack Koch's backhand and to poach to the net after serving.

The final day of the tie against Brazil, 6 December remains one of the most disappointing days of my life, in regard to my match against Mandarino. After having put up a valiant fight from the very beginning, I lost the match in a five setter, which I still think, I could have clinched. The final score line of 9-7, 3-6, 6-4, 3-6, 7-5, in favour of Mandarino probably provides you an imaginary glimpse of what really happened during the course of the match and tells everyone that the match could have gone any way. The final set of the match disappointed me the most as I was 4-3 up, with new balls to serve, in order to make it 5-3, but I lost the game and the score became 4-4, of which Mandarino took full advantage. Reflecting back to that particular game, it dawns upon me, that probably in order to please and impress, the home crowd with a win, I had played a game which was a little defensive, against an opponent who was ready to take more risk and play an all-out game, negating a few previous calculations.

It was now upon the shoulder of Ramanathan Krishnan to pave our way to Melbourne.

As Krishnan came on to the court to challenge Thomaz Koch on that sunny Sunday afternoon, the entire arena was pulsating with excitement, anxiety and anticipation. Though Koch took the first set rather easily, Krishnan came to his elements from the second set onwards. Winning the second set quite easily, Krishnan conveyed to Koch, who was the favourite for the match, that he too was playing against a Master. The third set, consisting of 22 games, turned out to be quite a rip-roarer, which Krishnan finally lost.

After the end of the third set, it was decided by the officials and umpires to carry forward the match to the next day, as the light was not conducive for further play. It was December in east India. This is something that does not often happen in Davis Cup, but the intensity of the competition between the two teams were such, that this exception had to be made. So, now the final fate of the tie was to be decided on a Monday morning.

From very early morning on Monday, there was a lot of buzz around the city and even the country (which I later came to know) as to who would have the winning match. Krishnan left the Grand Hotel, where he was staying, early in the morning and made his way to the Kalighat Temple, before arriving at South Club, looking fresh and composed, as always. Little did we know till then, that we were about to witness sheer magic for the next two sets – to be set up by a magician named Ramanathan Krishnan. So, when after the final point, the Magician threw his racquet towards the sky (an unusual demonstration of emotion from him) and was lifted up on their shoulders by two linesmen, Anwar Ali and Narendra Singh, I quietly got up from my seat to bow my head to the Almighty even as the crowd saluted the Godfather of India's tennis.

It is for the statistician to tell us, but I think this was India's first entry into the Finals of a World Cup event, for any sport. As a mark of this momentous occasion, the then Chief Minister of West Bengal, Prafulla Chandra Sen declared a State Holiday on 8 December.

● Full story, P. 13.   Krishnan returns with a backhand (right) and (below) watches a little later as his partner Mukerjea does the same.

THE FINALS OF the Davis Cup or the Challenge Round, as it was called then, was scheduled from 26 to 28 December at Kooyong Stadium in Melbourne.

Therefore, we actually had very little time to prepare ourselves for the Big Tie, against the cyclone that was the Australian Tennis Team, led by none other than Harry Hopman (also written as Hoffman, considered by many as one of greatest Tennis coaches who ever walked the planet) as the non-playing Captain. The team included legends like Fred Stolle, Roy Emerson, John Newcombe and Tony Roche as players, names that shall always be written in gold in the chronicles of Tennis History.

Team India for the Finals included Krishnan, Premjit, S P Misra (who joined us is Melbourne from Bangkok, where he happened to be representing India at the Asian Games) and myself. Akthar Ali, I believe, was unfairly dropped from the squad by the Federation. A man who has contributed immensely to Indian tennis, R K Khanna, was appointed to be the non-playing Captain for this historic tie.

Despite the fact that we were the underdogs, Krishnan and I believed that a bad day for any of the Australian players could create an upset, favouring us. I had beaten Fred Stolle in a tournament in Beckenham, England, just before the Wimbledon in the previous year and Krishnan's records against many of the top players in the world were also quite impressive. Hence, confidence was not missing in the team at all, though we knew very well, things were going to be pretty tough.

Finally, Premjit and I took off for Chennai around ten days before the tie, where Krishnan joined us and we flew in to Singapore. We had two nights of lay over in Singapore. In Singapore, we were warmly hosted by the Indian High Commission. An official dinner for the Indian team members, along with officials of the Australian High Commission, was arranged by the Indian High Commissioner in Singapore in order to foster goodwill and friendship among the two countries, which still happens to be the ethos of the Davis Cup.

Melbourne also welcomed us warmly, with its temperate weather and warm hospitality. We were put up in a very cozy hotel named Southern Cross, in the central area of the city, about five miles away from the venue. Australia, in general, is a sport lovers' country and however fierce they maybe on court, they are otherwise a remarkably amiable and genial people. The only fly in the ointment, for us, happened to be the Australian press which kept publishing demoralising headlines like 'Lambs to be Slaughtered'.

As our matches were to begin the day after Christmas, on Boxing Day, we took to gruelling practice sessions at the venue's practice courts. We were determined to get acclimatised to the conditions as much as possible, within the few days that we had before the tie. On this particular occasion, the Indian Team was also fortunate to have the support of Neale Frazer and my dear friend, Arthur Ashe (who was present in Melbourne due to his commitments in the Australian Circuit), at the practice sessions. These two great players with experience lend us their valuable support and encouragement.

Arthur, in fact, drove the Indian Team in his car to the tea party that was hosted by the Governor General of Melbourne and pretended to be the chauffer of the Indian Squad, when stopped at the gates. Such was the magnanimity of this Great Man. These are some of the unforgettable moments that Tennis has offered me, beyond score lines, championships and trophies, which I now want to share with my readers.

On Christmas morning, the draw took place in the Center Court of Kooyong Stadium, which determined that Fred would take on Krishnan in the first match. I would have to play Roy Emerson (the Australian Open Champion of 1966 and the record holder for winning the maximum number of this championship in the Amateur years) in the second match.

The first day of the tie proved to be a bit of a let-down for India. Both, Krishnan and I, lost in straight sets but not before putting up a commendable fight, much to the delight and surprise of the ten thousand plus spectators at the Kooyong Stadium, the ground which became the permanent venue for the Australian Open from 1972 to 1987. We were determined to come back the next day, with greater valour.

Little did we realise at the beginning of the second day, when the Indian Doubles pair of Krishnan and Mukerjea took to the court against Newcombe and Roche (a pair who had not lost a single match that year and went on to make the podium finish in three slams, the next year) that I would soon become a reference point in the national Davis Cup folklore.

In spite of losing the first set of this crucial Doubles match, we still kept our spirits soaring high and began the second set on a very positive note, vowing to go all out. In our heads played the slogan: we are no way less than the Aussies. We decided to keep the return of serves as precise as possible, and, I was given the task to poach, as often as possible. Thus began the saga of three straight sets and, the match, in our favour. The final scores read: 4-6, 7-5, 6-4, 6-4.

It was possibly one of the biggest upsets in world tennis at that time and an archival tale for Indian Tennis.

A unique experience that we had in this match, I have never experienced in my life as a player, or otherwise. We received wholehearted cheer and support from the watching crowd in an away-match (that is outside of one's own country), that we Indians had never witnessed before. We knew our exemplary courage and display of world-class tennis had earned us this accolade from the extremely competitive Aussies and the

Australian viewership. I still remember, Tony Roche's words during a changeover: 'Hey, are we playing in Australia or India?' Remember 1966 was before the advent of Indian cricket and the kudos we received was unprecedented for those times.

Now it was Krishnan's turn to take on the legend called Roy Emerson in the first match of the penultimate day. Roy was in a fiery form at that time, but Krishnan also held the distinction of defeating Roy at the Quarter-finals of Wimbledon in 1961. Although not really evenly poised, we still 'Hoped for the Best'. On this occasion, Roy proved to be more powerful and precise, thus, shattering our dreams of lifting the Davis Cup for India. A dream that I cherish even today and firmly believe, one day, it will be a reality.

Upholding the resolve with which we had arrived at Melbourne – of not letting our opponents win a single point without a fight, I started the tie's last match against Fred Stolle, which turned out to be Stolle's last match in Davis Cup, as he had decided to join the Professional Tennis Circuit from the beginning of the following year and thus would be barred from playing Davis Cup. Woefully, in this encounter, even after stretching the match to five sets (7-5, 6-8, 6-3, 5-7, 6-3) and winning the hearts of the crowd and the media, I was not able to get the better of Stolle.

The result of the tie came off to be 4-1, on the side of the Australians. However, even after so many years, I can resolutely assure all, we bade adieu to Melbourne with our heads held high and with a silent proclamation – Indian Tennis has arrived on the world stage and is here to remain, for a long, long time.

Chapter 7

CAPTAINING TEAM INDIA FOR THE DAVIS CUP

I TOOK OVER the captaincy of Team India for the Davis Cup from Naresh Kumar in 1993. In the previous year, India had performed well, losing to Australia. After the tie, our no. 1 player Ramesh Krishnan decided to retire from the Davis Cup competition.

As a result, I inherited a very young squad with relatively no Davis Cup exposure. Only Leander Paes had played some great matches. Crafting a team is a difficult proposition for any game and any captain.

Our first tie was against the formidable US team in Delhi; the US team consisted of world no 1 Jim Courier and others and playing them was a tough task. Nevertheless, the Indian team played well and we lost 5-0.

This was a learning experience for me. Therefore, in the next tie against South Africa, the team assembled two weeks earlier for a camp in Jaipur. I also invited US inter-collegiate player Mahesh Bhupathi to join the camp, as he was making waves in the Challenger Circuit of the Association of Tennis Professionals (ATP). Mahesh was there with eight other boys and he played very well, improving tremendously after I talked to him about his game. At the end of the camp, Mahesh Bhupathi was playing the best and was winning all his practice matches. I was in a quandary, and didn't know who to select as the fourth member in the team. Finally, I decided after much deliberation to include Bhupathi and leave out Zeeshan Ali. I saw Mahesh's talent and knew that he will be the future star of Indian tennis. And he proved me right.

I knew Mahesh's father very well, first. He was a good national level tennis player; I think he played in the squad and he went to work in Muscat. Mahesh was born there, he was a heavy boy as a child. I saw him play in the Challenger tournament, and he did very well in the South-East Asia tournament. In the Jaipur camp too, he was beating Zeeshan regularly. So, I decided, we needed a young guy like him who was still raw, so I picked him up and put him in the team with Leander, Gaurav Natekar and another player.

When I chose a rookie like Mahesh Bhupathi, I was severely criticised but at the end of the day, you are the captain and you have to take the pressure. He is your responsibility. You are the captain of the ship; no one tells you what to do, you have to take the tough call; so, I did it and I did what I thought was right and I was successful and I was right because today, people know where was Mahesh Bhupathi's tennis at that time compared to all others.

The Secretary of the All-India Tennis Association, R K Khanna asked me to rethink my decision but I was adamant to have Mahesh in the team and in retrospect, now you can see that my decision that day was the right decision.

When I announced the team, all hell broke loose. My good friend Akhtar Ali stopped talking to me and the press and media began to hound me to find out why I had dropped Zeeshan; more so as Zeeshan was from my Kolkata club, the South Club and the son of my friend Akhtar. This brought about a rift between us, but being top sportsmen, we decided to overlook the incident.

After the South Africa tie, I convinced Leander to play some tournaments with Mahesh and they did really well and that's how the Indian Express of Leander and Mahesh started. They have won many grand slam Doubles titles together and if they had continued their partnership, they would have won many more.

My captaincy did not start too well, as I mentioned earlier. We played against the USA and then South Africa, which we lost. Perhaps we needed a good second Singles player.

In the next year we won the Asian group easily and then we had to play Croatia in the world group play off. We were lucky as we were playing them in Delhi. Once again, Leander won both his Singles matches and the Doubles with Mahesh.

I think Leander played amazing tennis when he beat Wimbledon champion Goran Ivanesivic. We all called him Davis Cup Paes as he always played better in Davis Cup for his country. We were mainly playing in the world group where the best 16 teams play. We played some great ties, losing some close ties against Sweden, UK, Italy and the Czech Republic. We also won two ties against Chile and the Netherlands. We could have won the tie against Italy but unfortunately, Leander did not play as he was nursing a bad shoulder. However, I kept his place open and requested him to at least play the Doubles but he did not come and we lost 3/1. Had he played, we would have surely won. The funny part is, the next week, he played the Indian Open in Chennai and reached the semi-finals!

As a player, there is a disappointment if you are not selected or are not good enough to play. However, one keeps such disappointments to one's own self. One is in the same team and no one wants to hurt the other players.

I am sure Premjit Lall too was disappointed when he was not selected to play in 1965-66. I used to play Singles and I played more second Singles than Premjit because the then captain had more confidence in me... not because I was a better player but because I performed better under pressure and I was able to lift my game. Some players are able to lift better their game under pressure and I was able to do that and that gave me many wins. That is why the non-playing captains favoured me.

Leander was a Calcutta boy, he trained at the South Club. He played at the CCFC. His father was a good friend of mine. Later, when Vijay Amritraj started a training camp called the BAT Britannia Amritraj Tennis Training Scheme for 12–13-year-old age group in Chennai, Leander went there. They selected juniors from India and they had a lot of finance and they had a lot of foreign coaches coming and staying in

Chennai. The young players would stay together and they would go to school together. They practised together and among the players that came out of that academy were Leander Paes, Gaurav Natekar, Asif Ismail and Rohit Rajpal. If we had more academies like this in India, it would surely help the sport, help tennis.

I captained the Davis Cup team from 1993-1999 and I think I did quite a good job.

I was the non-playing captain of the Indian tennis team to the Atlanta Olympics in 1996, where Leander Paes won the bronze medal in Singles which was an amazing feat – the first individual medal won by any Indian athlete since 1947.

All in all, I feel I have done well as a captain. All the boys under me did well in the international circuit and the icing on the cake was when Leander and Mahesh won the Wimbledon Doubles title for the first time. I was there watching and I couldn't control my tears after their victory.

When I call Mahesh today, even now he immediately picks up the call and talks. Mahesh is genuine, warm.

I really enjoyed my stint as captain and I think all the boys who played under me had a huge respect for me.

Jaidip with Leander Paes.

Jaidip with Mahesh Bhupathi.

Chapter 8

TALKING TENNIS

THE GRANDSLAMS ARE the ultimate tournaments. Grand slams are the four biggest tournaments of the world – the four ultimate championships which are the Wimbledon championship in London; the French championship in Paris; the Australian championship in Melbourne and the US Open in New York and every top player tries to participate in these.

Next, we have the smaller tournaments that lead to the Grand Slams. Now there is prize money in sports – $250,000 prize money for the Semis and $500,00 for the Grand Slam. For me, the first goal was to win the Wimbledon and second came any other Grand Slam. Now you have the ATP points for men and WTA points for women; they are two separate organisations that together handle the game of world tennis with other organisations.

I went to England in 1959 as a 17-year-old and played Junior Wimbledon and Senior Wimbledon, both. So, for me, my favourite grand slam tournament is Wimbledon. My year

usually started with the Australian Open because our winter is their summer in December-January, followed by the French Open in May and Wimbledon in July. Last came the US Open in early September-October.

Everyone has some weakness or the other. Tactics is when you know someone's weaknesses, know that so-and so's backhand is weak. Some people cannot move forward but on Clay Court, you have to be physically very strong if you are playing a 4-5 hour match. A lot depends on the coaches' foresight, how they train.

I remember we were training for a Davis Cup match in Mexico in November, I think. It was in the year when the war with China happened, 1962. We had an Australian coach, Stan Edwards. He was a very nice guy but he was a strict disciplinarian and he wanted us to run on the road. A friend had told me don't run on the tarmac road, your legs will get heavy, especially on the road or the sand. It is fine if you're running off-season. But during season, when Edwards said, run on the road, I did not want to. He could not understand why I was reluctant. We argued, I tried to explain, but he was the coach, so we ran on the road.

Sure enough, when I was playing the match – at the

beginning I was good stamina-wise but all of a sudden, my legs felt so heavy, they nearly gave away. I felt a pain on my calf, which had never happened to me before. Later, when I told the coach what had happened, he said no, this could not be. Later he said sorry and it was okay. However, Krishnan refused to run on the tarmacked road; he was adamant. To please the coach, I, Premjit and Akhtar ran on the road. I think that was a downfall in hindsight. In the next match I was leading 5-2 set against Antonio Palafox. I think we could've won the tie, but I had just crashed.

I think Indians don't do well in Clay because physically now, they are not strong enough.

The reason is that we don't train on slow courts. The only two Clay Courts are in Calcutta's Saturday Club and the South Club. Tolly Club has brick-clay. The courts in India are all brick-clay. Earlier, we had Vijay Amritraj who did well in Wimbledon; Ramesh Krishnan did very well in Wimbledon; but only Ramanathan Krishnan and I got to the pre-Quarter and Quarter-final. I got to the pre-Quarter in the French twice; and Krishnan got to the Quarter-final once – so, apart from that, no one in India has really reached that round. In our days on grass court the ball used to be lighter, now it is heavier so that the match is longer for the spectators.

My ambition from the beginning was to be a sportsman but there was no money in sports in our time compared to what there is now. So, it was a catch 22 situation. No money, how does one play, how does one travel?

Fortunately for us, the secretary of the club arranged

Vijay Amritraj with Ramesh Krishnan.

matches for us where State level tournaments would take place. As far as the juniors were concerned, we used to get a 2nd class or 3rd class train fare and free stay, boarding and lodging. Senior players would get better boarding, but there was no prize money as such. We, however, got to play a big tournament in Bombay and got Rs 4,000, which was a lot of money in those days. Every player had a rate. We had a lot of foreigners coming in – the English and the East Europeans. They could not go to South Africa in the winters, because of apartheid rules and they came to practise in India. All top champions came to India. For practice, they played with us and that's how we managed.

FOR AN ATHLETE who is aspiring to be pro, there are a lot of ups and downs. You lose more matches than you win; even the best players in the world, they lose more than they win and they may not like it.

Unfortunately, in our days, we did not have many people travelling with us. We couldn't afford it. We had coaches at home and Dilip Bose was our coach in India. But he didn't travel with us. We had to travel alone and fend for ourselves. This was very unfortunate. I am sure that if I and Premjit had proper coaches advising us, we would be 25 to 35 per cent better players than we were. We actually didn't know how to work out, what exercise to do... there was a taboo on weight lifting, weight training. The body gets too stiff playing just one kind of game. We ran around the race course and did sprints etcetera, that's how we kept ourselves fit and there was no coach telling us what exactly to do. Some days we slept late, had we a coach with us, he would have chased us about exercises and practice. Unfortunately, we didn't have good coaching like sports persons have today. I am sure players of our generation would have done very well... I mean we did pretty well at the international level but we could have done better.

We had a coach in Akhtar Ali after Dilip Bose. However, he was not a coach as such but a friend. In those days, I was just a player. I was not involved at that time in selections etc. The captain decided with the manager who to play, but off and on, Premjit and I would have some arguments and difference of opinion about the Doubles matches. These were generally regarding... 'I should have done this' or 'you should have done that' and then I would at times say, shut up, it happens naa… tennis not being a team game as such, in this, one did not depend on others, one depended on one's own self. It is a game where you… uh… just have to carry on if your partner in Doubles is not playing well. You have to carry him. And if you're not playing well, he has to carry you.

In Singles you are all alone. If you lose a match, it's your fault or the other guy is a better player or played better than you that day. What really hurts sometimes when you lose matches is when you get cheated… a wrong call will go against you, a ball might fall on the line and the umpire might call out and that makes a lot of difference. This did not happen often. But once or twice it did happen.

Once, in Wimbledon, I was playing Pierre Darmon. The French number 1 was playing at Wimbledon at the 3rd round and we were one set all, and he was supposed to be serving. I was leading 40 -15 and he served a double fault on the side. Clearly, it was out and the umpire didn't see it, so he gave the point to Darmon. I argued, I lost my temper with the umpire, I was right. But then… the umpire's decision was final as always. He didn't change his mind and I lost that game. But I went on to win the set and finally win the match.

Sometimes, these wrong calls lift you up, but it can also go the other way and crush you. If I didn't have that… I would've lost the match but, in my case, the umpire got me so annoyed that in anger, I played furiously and really lifted my game to beat Darmon. He was a really good player. At that time, when I was playing him, he was better than me.

Sports Injuries

INJURY IS A WORD, which can literally cause anxiety and panic attacks amongst most sportspersons. There have been numerous instances, where due to injury related issues, a sports person had to take an early exit from his or her sporting career.

During my playing days, I have had my share of injuries too, but with God's grace, no surgery or major lay off from the field was ever required. My injuries came early in my career, teaching me many lessons on what not to do, which perhaps is one of the reasons why, in later years, I have been relatively injury-free.

Novak Djokovic

My first experience with injury, which haunts me even today, is when I had to give a walk-over to Ronny Barnes (of Brazil), in the Semi-finals of Junior Wimbledon in 1959, after having defeated the top seed, J L Arilla of Spain in the Quarter-finals. It was really a heart-breaking episode, especially for a seventeen-year-old lad. I had put in all I had to offer in the Quarter-finals, thus twisting my ankle in the process. Though I managed to win, my ankle subsequently became worse, making it impossible for me to stand on court for the Semi-finals.

Again, during the US Summer Circuit of 1962, my back started to hurt me, and after a few tournaments, it became quite unbearable. Someone then suggested trying sleeping on the floor. As luck would have it, I got miraculously cured, just before the US Open, where I reached the last sixteen of a Grand Slam, for the second time in my career, before losing to Rafael Osuna of Mexico.

Pierre Darmon   **Ronny Barnes**   **J L Arilla**   **Rafael Osuna**

1966 was the year which gave me much joy and satisfaction as a player. India managed to reach the Challenge Round of Davis Cup for the first time, and I as an individual player reached the last 16 of 2 Grand Slams (Wimbledon & French Open). But, this was also the year in which my right shoulder gave me a lot of trouble, by remaining sore, and thus causing great discomfort. Cortisone injections had to be administered, quite often, to ward off the pain.

Therefore, as a player who has spent nearly two decades in the professional circuit, I would like to make a few humble suggestions to all sportspersons, whether amateur or professional, regarding prevention of injuries:

First of all, take the help of a doctor or a sports clinic, to 'Evaluate your Body'. Each individual has a different set of strengths or weaknesses in his or her body, which should be ascertained, as early as possible, before embarking on a training schedule.

Secondly, I would suggest, players perusing one kind of sport try their hands in other kind of sports too. This tends to break the monotony, and also helps in creating strength, flexibility, agility and concentration, which can be of great help, even when one is perusing or specialising in some other sporting event. Like, I learnt to play tennis but I also played cricket and rugby and squash and several other games throughout school, and later on too.

Wooden Racquets

IN OUR DAYS we played with wooden racquets and this caused lot of injuries in the wrist, elbow and shoulder; some great players have had to give up the game because of this. However, with the advent of titanium and graphite racquets the injuries are far less, so the modern day professional players do not have many nagging pains.

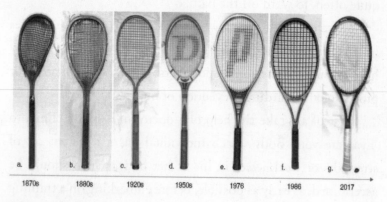

a.	b.	c.	d.	e.	f.	g.
1870s	1880s	1920s	1950s	1976	1986	2017

IN NATIONALS, I recall some of my rivals who were good players. When I first started playing junior U12 and U14, there was a guy called Alok Mitra from north Calcutta. I was better than him but we had close matches. Then came Premjit Lall and Akhtar Ali. Premjit had beaten me as a youngster, so it was a great thing to beat him. Akhtar was older than me, he used to beat me earlier. Then I started beating him.

Next thing was to beat Ramanathan Krishnan who was India's best and World number 3 and he was absolutely a great player. The first time I beat him was in the Asian Championships held in Calcutta in January 1966, in the famous grass courts of Calcutta South Club.

There was no bad blood among players though. When the match was over, players shook hands and you were friends again, although that doesn't happen in life.

In the international circuit, I would say, Bob Hewitt from Australia was a rival. Then there was Ken Fletcher, Tony Roche, John Newcombe... all the top players. There was a club called the Last 8 Club in Wimbledon. We used to talk and chat, have dinner there... it was for the players who reached the last eight positions at Wimbledon.

When you go to a restaurant and have dinner, and you win the next match, you want to go back to the same restaurant so that you win again. This is a ritual like playing in the match-winning shirt again and again. In tennis, like in all other sports, there are a few rituals. Once, I remember I was playing the Semi-finals in the same year in Junior Wimbledon and near the place we stayed in, there was a street and a ladder and a guy was working on the ladder. That time, I had not noticed the ladder and I went right through under it. Later, I recalled, going under the ladder is very unlucky. So, after I had crossed the ladder, I thought I would not win the match. Nevertheless, I went and I won the match later.

Sledging charges never plagued me, but I know for a fact that there was a huge hue and cry when we were playing in Berlin. Bob Hewitt was playing Roger Taylor. Taylor won the match and there were a lot of arguments on court and the temperamental Aussie said, 'come outside, I'll show you'. After they finished the match, they went back to the dressing room and a young boy came to Hewitt for an autograph.

BH told him, 'Why do you want my autograph, take that crook's autograph'. Then a fist fight broke out between them. And BH couldn't play the next couple of weeks. He was bad tempered and no one liked him.

AFTER MY FIRST Wimbledon season, I became a regular player in the world tennis circuit. From 1960 to 1974, I played all the Grand Slam tournaments such as the Wimbledon, the French Open, the US Open and the Australian Open. In Australia and USA there was no money in the Opens and they were strictly amateur, so one did not find any top players from Europe and other places going there.

MUKERJEA ENTERS SEMI-FINAL

Lall Goes Down To Roy Emerson

PERTH, Nov. 29.—Jaideep Mukerjea, of India, stormed into the men's singles semi-final at the West Australian Lawn Tennis Championships here today. reports Reuter

In the quarter-finals. Mukerjea beat Wilhelm Bungert, of West Germany, 6-3, 6-2.

Premjit Lall, the other Indian representative in the last eight, went out to Australia's Roy Emerson. who won 6-4, 6-2.

In the remaining quarter-finals, Neale Fraser beat John Newcombe, the Australian junior champion. 6-2 6-2 and Fletcher beat R. Brent. 2-6, 6-3, 6-3

Mukerjea and Lall were beaten in the men's doubles quarter-finals by Fletcher and Newcombe. The young Australians won 3-6, 6-3. 6-2.

Australians Roy Emerson and Neale Fraser beat compatriots Clive Walderspin and Rob Kilderry 6-0. 6-4 to reach the doubles semi-finals.

MUKERJEA AND LAL WIN AT SYDNEY

SYDNEY. Nov. 13.—India had two successes when the New South Wales Lawn Tennis Championships got under way here today, reports Reuter.

In the first round of the men's singles Jaideep Mukerjea beat O Davidson 7-9, 7-5, 6-2 and P. Lal defeated P. McPherson 4-6, 6-3, 6-2.

The world tennis circuit was quite different in those days as there was no prize money. The Australian circuit used to be held in December-January, very few overseas players used to go there as it was very far and with no prize money.

The South African circuit was at the same time as the Indian circuit, and mainly players from Australia and USA played in this circuit. Due to anti-apartheid sanctions, East European players and Indian players did not participate in this circuit. However, the most prestigious circuit in those days was the Caribbean circuit, where everyone wanted to play as the appearance money was very good; so was the five-star hospitality. The circuit started with the US Indoor in Salisbury, Maryland tournaments and then carried on to Tampa, Miami, Trinidad, Caracas, Bogota, San Juan, Puerto Rico and finished in Mexico City. I had the privilege to play this circuit twice and have some great memories, especially in San Juan, Caracas and Bogota.

The Indian circuit started in early December and went on till March. We had a lot of European players, especially East Europeans playing the circuit. Names such as Nastase, Jan Kodeš , Teriac and others played the Indian circuit regularly.

Nastase   **Teriac**

The Indian circuit was very well organised and started with the typical grass court tournaments and ended with the national championships and then the clay court circuit, that happened in then Bombay and went on to tournaments in Indore, Trivandrum, Bangalore and Chennai. I was a regular player from my junior days in this circuit for many years and thoroughly enjoyed my stay in different parts of India.

Unlike today's ITF tournaments and ATP tournaments where they only give prize money, in our time we used to get some appearance money, travel expenses and free board and lodging, even if you were a junior player.

In December 1961, Premjit and I were sent to Australia to play the Australian circuit and train under the legendary Australian coach Harry Hopman, who has produced many champions like Rod Laver, Lew Hoad, Ken Rosewell, Roy Emerson, John Newcombe and others.

The first tournament we played was in Brisbane and that's where I learnt Australians have steak and eggs for breakfast. I lost in the second round in Brisbane and Sydney, but I reached the semi-finals in Adelaide and Perth. In Adelaide, in the Semis, I played Neale Frazer and the other Semi-finals was between Laver and Emerson. You can imagine how I felt playing in the semi-finals where the other three players were all Wimbledon champions. It was really nerve-wracking.

In December 1961, I reached the last 16 of the Australian Open, losing to Roy Emerson. In the Australian circuit I have beaten players such as Ken Flecther, Bob Hewitt, W Bungert of Germany and others. The Australian tour and training under

Harry Hopman did me a world of good, it gave me confidence to take on any top player in the world. Physically too, I became much stronger. I wish I had the opportunity to go back again in November 1962, because I am sure another stint with Hopman would have made me a better player. For aspiring tennis players all over the world, the main tournament to win or even to participate in was Wimbledon in our days and that was the ultimate favourite of tennis players.

The Tatas Sponsorship

IN FEBRUARY 1962, something changed in my life, when for the first time I could concentrate fully on my tennis and I became a better player.

At an official sit-down dinner party at the Willingdon Club in Bombay, I was seated next to a dignified elderly Parsi lady who was very kind and friendly. She asked me what I was doing and what I will do in the near future. I was in college then and told her that after graduating, I would probably join a tea company in Kolkata and become a Boxwala, which was the route those days for young men. She asked me, 'What

will happen to your tennis?' I told her that tennis would have to take a back seat as I had to look after my future.

I did not know at that time that this charming lady was Rodaben, the sister of J R D Tata, chairman of Tata Sons and the wife of Colonel Leslie

Sawhney, Chairman of Tata Chemicals and the Taj Group of Hotels. She spoke to her brother JRD, and her husband, about me and Premjit and after a couple of days, I and Premjit had a meeting with Colonel Sawhney and Dharmsey Khatau, head of the Khatau Group, along with J Charanjiva, then India's Number 1 tennis player, who was also the president of the International Lawn Tennis Club of India.

At this meeting, these high-profile elders decided that Premjit would join the ACC Cement Company and I would join Tata Steel in Kolkata. After a couple of months, when we thought nothing was going to happen, I suddenly got a letter from Tata Steel when I was playing at Wimbledon. I was really shocked, surprised and happy to get this appointment letter.

I was recruited as a section officer starting at a salary of Rs 650, which was in those days, for us like a lakh of rupees. Premjit and I were allowed to play all the tennis we wanted while our salaries went to the bank, and the only condition was that when we were in Kolkata, we had to go to our respective offices to learn to work.

I was initially attached to the coal department of Tata Steel and my big boss was none other than the flamboyant and great Russi Mody. It was a great experience to work for Tata Steel under Mody, he was a very good boss and encouraged my tennis. He too was a good club player and used to play regularly at the South Club. I remember, I used to go to the coal mines in Dhanbad and go underground and see the miners at work and learnt a lot about coal. I made some good friends in Tata during my time, among them Anwar Hasan who became a director of Tatas in London. Another friend was K C Mehra who tried his hand in acting at Bombay, and cricketers Prakash Bhandari, S S Mitra, Sushil Kapoor and many others. It was a very happy and exciting time for me.

Spirit of the Game

IN THE ROLAND GARROS, the French Open, I reached the last 16 twice; on both occasion I lost to Roy Emerson twice who was World Number 1 in those days and it was pretty good for me to get to the last 16 of the French Open. It is very tough to play in France on very slow clay courts; one has got to be very strong and fit and we had to literary grind our way during the match. I consider that record – getting to the last 16 in the Roland Garros – as good as getting to the last 16 at Wimbledon. I am the only Indian, apart from Ramanathan Krishnan, who reached the Quarters in the Roland Garros. The other Indians after us like Vijay Amritraj, Ramesh Kirshnan and others never got to the last 16 because the surface is very slow and it is very tough to play on it.

In the US Open, I have played the first season in grass four-five times; I got to the last 16 in 1962, where Rod Laver won his Grand Slam. I lost in the last 16 to the Mexican Rafael Osuna who was a fantastic player. Unfortunately, he died young in a plane crash. I lost to Osuna, but it was a good match and I had several chances but he beat me in 4 sets.

In the third round I played Charlie Pasarell from the USA, who was of Puerto Rican origin. He had had a fantastic grass court session that year and was doing really well in the

Rod Laver

tournament in the US. I was playing in the 3rd round on a very hot and humid day in my last tournament in the US before returning home and he won the first set. I won the second, he won the third and I was tired. In those days, we took a break after the third set, so when I went into a break that day, I was just thinking about home and my night flight back to India.

When we got back on court, I lost my serve in the first game then, all of a sudden, I don't know what actually happened – I just saw the tennis ball as a football and played fantastic tennis, which I had never played before. Whatever I did just came in –

amazing tennis, in fact. Charlie Pasarell was very shocked and he began shouting at me, 'what are you doing to me, what you doing to me Jay, what is this!'

Charlie and I are very old friends and go back a long way, he is a very nice person and a very big businessman in Puerto Rico and he owns the tournament Indian Wells Masters, which I said earlier is one of the best ATP tournaments and tour, so that was one of my best years of tennis.

After that, I played Cliff Riche and several others. One incident that comes to my mind is when the Tie-breaker first started, it was in the US Open and it was a sudden death trial which means, in the 4th or 5th set, players get a tie-breaker 6-All and one gets just 1 point to finish the match.

I was playing Hank Erwin of Rhodesia (now Zimbawbe) in the 2nd round I think, I led in 2 sets to 1, I won the first set 7-6, he won the second set 7-6, I won the 3rd set 7-6 and in the 4th set we were 6 games All, 6 points All, and after the last point, it was decided that I or he would win the match, whosoever won the 1st set. It was his service and it was on a grass court and the odds were with him. I, however, had a choice – the choice of receiving either on the forehand court or the backhand court. I took the forehand court and he served the first service fault. In the second serve, I decided, no matter what happens, I would run around and hit my forehand. As he served, I ran around to hit my forehand and as luck would have it he served a double fault. I was never so relieved in my life – to win a match like that, it was simply amazing! And that's what the tie-breaker does.

Jimmie Van Allen

Nowadays you have the tie breaker which carries on and on and on for this sudden death. The system was introduced by a Newport Island businessman called Jimmie Van Allen and, in those days, the scoring system for that tournament was called the VASS Van Allen Scoring System. His work has been showcased by the writer Eleanor Dwight in a book called, *Tie Breaker: Jimmy Van Alen and Tennis in the 20th Century.*

I really admire the Indian guys who won medals at the Commonwealth Games – that is because the government right now is supporting them.

WHEN I RECEIVED the Arjuna Award in 1967, another person who was awarded Arjuna Award with me was a weight lifter. He had no money, no resources, he was selling peanuts in New Delhi station. In other countries this doesn't happen. I don't recollect his name. I was given a third-class ticket to travel, after the awards ceremony. Those small things rankle. Sports in the 1960s, '70s was considered a *theek ache* thing (okay, good, that's it), nothing big. There was no requisite respect for sportsmen in India. Sports of any kind is a very tough profession and that

भारत सरकार
युवा कार्यक्रम और खेल मंत्रालय
सर्व श्रेष्ठ खिलाड़ी के लिये अर्जुन पुरस्कार
1966 (द्वितीय प्रति)

यह अर्जुन पुरस्कार श्री जयदीप मुकर्जी को प्रदान किया जाता है जिन्हें लॉन टेनिस में वर्ष का सर्वश्रेष्ठ खिलाड़ी घोषित किया गया है।

GOVERNMENT OF INDIA
Ministry of Youth Affairs & Sports

ARJUNA AWARD FOR BEST SPORTSPERSON
1966

This Arjuna Award is given to *Shri Jaidip Mukerjea* who has been declared the best sportsperson of the year in *Lawn Tennis*

नई दिल्ली
New Delhi
दिनांक : दिसम्बर 30, 2002
Dated December 30, 2002

(एल. एम. मेहता)
(L. M. MEHTA)
सचिव
Secretary
भारत सरकार
to the Government of India

ITF

Award for Services to the Game

Presented by the
International Tennis Federation
to

Jaidip Mukerjea

India

In Recognition of
Long and Distinguished Service
To the Game of Tennis

Francesco Ricci Bitti
President

September 2003

requires determination and makes one very strong. In our days, there was no one to push us. We trained, true, but no one told us 'lets go, lets go, do this... do that'. In my case, I was very strong physically. I was into rugby, football and other sports. Each game helps... each game builds you up and makes you more coordinated... like, if you're a football player your legs are stronger if you're also a squash player. You have good stamina. Each sport complements the other sport.

TENNIS ALSO GAVE many of us the opportunity to hear some great music live. We grew up with Beatles, Rolling Stones and I've heard their concerts live in London and I also have had the opportunity to meet Mick Jagger. I have met other singers like Cliff Richards and the Bee Gees. Much later, I saw Tom Jones at Las Vegas.

Once in New York, we were practicing at the Forest Hill Stadium in the morning, courtesy the West Side Tennis Club. This was before the US championship. The security guy told us that we had to clear out before 1 'o clock because the Beatles were coming to perform there at a concert later.

The Beatles! Surely, we wanted to hear the Beatles. The security guy said, 'you want to hear them, then stay put in the stadium... don't go out'. So, Premjit, I and a few other players stayed put there and as the club where they performed was the West Side Tennis Club, we saw and heard them live. It was amazing to hear them and see the massive crowd and the frenzy and all those teenagers – all young people, fifteen-sixteen-year-old girls and guys – it was one of the most fantastic experiences I have had.

Yes, tennis took me places and to people.

Chapter 9

THE THREE MUSKETEERS OF INDIAN TENNIS

IN THE 1960S, we were nick-named 'The Three Musketeers' of Indian tennis – meaning Ramanathan Krishnan, Premjit Lall and Jaideep Mukerjea (KLM). When we lost early in tournaments, tennis fans called us the 'Three Mosquitoes'.

Premjit Lall

Premjit Lall was the best player in our South Club coaching group. He had all the shots, a good service, very good ground strokes and a decent volley, unfortunately his temperament was a little suspect.

Premjit hailed from Bhagalpur in Bihar but his family had settled in Kolkata and he did his schooling and college in Kolkata. You can say that he was more a Bengali than a Bihari. His father, Mahendar Lall, worked for Jessop & Co, one of the largest engineering companies in Asia. He retired as one of the directors of this prestigious company. He was very kind and soft-hearted and never interfered in Premjit's tennis choices like some of the parents do nowadays.

Like me, Premjit played Davis Cup for India for many years and also had some great wins in the international tennis circuit. Premjit won several tournaments abroad and was also the National Champion in the late '60s and '70s. Those days, either Prem or I would be the no.1 player in India. I could never beat him as a junior and finally managed to beat him in the Calcutta Hard Court tournament in 1958 and, this – for me this was a red-letter day.

I have seen Premjit play some great matches but the one that comes to my mind is the one against Rod Laver at Wimbledon in 1969, when Laver won the Grand Slam for the second time. In the second round, Premjit played Laver and led him 2 sets to Love and the games went with service till 4-All in the 3rd set. Premjit had the chance to win the match but unfortunately lost in the 5th set.

Nevertheless, he had played amazing tennis for the first two sets and whatever he tried went in, it was like Premjit had a magic wand in his hand. Laver still talks about this match.

Premjit played till 1979. His life after tennis was really tough and he went through some very bad times and even tried to commit suicide. It was sad to see a person who was doing so well in life and had everything going for him suddenly go into depression; he wanted to leave the world…I can't still imagine this. He died on 31 December 2008. I lost one of my closest and dearest friends, with whom I spent maybe half my life, travelling together, sharing wins and defeats, happy and sad moments. May his soul rest in peace.

The tennis fraternity of India, including the All-India Tennis Association and Bengal Tennis did not do very much for him. What a player, what a man – hats off to a great sporting personality that was Premjit Lall. For the last seven years, my wife Sharmin has taken it upon herself to organise a national-level tournament in the name of Premjit Lall at the Jaidip Mukerjea Tennis Academy in Kolkata where all the top-ranking players have played to honour the great Premjit Lall.

Ramanathan Krishnan

Ramanathan Krishnan – **Krish** as we all called him – was in my opinion the best player India has ever produced. He won the Men's Singles title at the Indian National Championship at the young age of 16 years, the youngest champion to do so. Krish's record proves he was the best, twice Singles Semi-finalist at Wimbledon and Quarter-finalist at the French Open at Roland Garros; winner of the US Hard Court, the Queen Club tournament at London which was a curtain-raiser for Wimbledon and umpteen

number of tournaments in the international circuit around the world. He has defeated all the top-ranking players of the world such as Rod Laver, Roy Emerson, Chuck McKinley and others.

Krishnan had tremendous stamina and never lost a match because of tiredness. All of us younger players looked up to him as our idol. He beat me so many times that my goal often was how to beat him. Also, he used to beat me very badly so that in future matches, I would have a fear, playing against him. Later on, when we became close friends and team mates, I once asked him why he used to do that. His answer was that he knew that Premjit and I were dangers to his top rank, therefore he tried to beat us as badly as possible to break our confidence.

I have played against Vijay Amritraj, Ramesh Krishnan and others, but Krish was in a different class altogether; he was solid and had no real weaknesses. When we were playing Davis Cup against any weaker side, we were sure that Krishnan would win his two Singles and we just had to win the Doubles to win the tie.

He was ranked no.3 in the world and he had reached Singles Semi-finals at Wimbledon in 1960 and again in 1961, where he lost to the eventual winners Neale Frazer and Rod Laver.

Krishnan won tournaments all around the world all the time. He was also a very good negotiator for his participation in various tournaments. I remember a time when I was playing in La Coruña, Spain when I heard about the sudden demise of his father-in law. Krish had to rush back to India and he was supposed to play a tournament in Quebec City, Canada in a couple of weeks. I asked him if I could go to the tournament in his place, he asked me to contact the organisers and they agreed and I went to play in Quebec in his place. At that time, I did not know what terms Krishnan had with them, but I readily agreed to the same terms Krishnan was getting. I knew it would be a good amount but I did not ask the organisers. Playing in Europe, I would usually get around $300 to $400, so you can imagine my surprise when I got a cheque for $2000 in Quebec, which is the highest I ever got from a tournament in those days. So, you can see, Krish was not only a great player but also a shrewd negotiator. I have a very healthy respect for him not only as a player but also as a great person.

Krish had a fantastic game, a great backhand and smash, amazing anticipation and also, he was physically very strong and never lost a match due to tiredness. He always liked a challenge and I was privileged to play with him. He was a great team mate and thanks to him, we won the famous Doubles match in the Davis Cup finals against Newcombe and Roche. Always ready to help his teammates, he gave valuable advice to the junior players. I have learnt so much from him in and outside the tennis court.

Jaidip Mukerjea

I, **Jaidip**, was the third musketeer. People say that I had a good match temperament and was a fighter till the last point; my strokes were not as good as the other two musketeers but my net game and overhead were my forte. Physically I was pretty fit and strong, which I attribute to my early days when I played cricket, hockey, football and rugby at a decent level which helped me in the long run.

When I was in my thirties, I had a shoulder problem and I was seeing experts and doctors. At that time, I was in great pain and I did think of leaving the game.

Another time I was depressed was in 1972-73 when I had accompanied a friend drinking on a court and the next day, the headlines said, Jaidip caught at the net. The incident made me very sad. Today, I have reconciled to the fact that no one can be perfect.

Chapter 10

MY PILLAR OF STRENGTH

I MET MY WIFE Sharmin when I was the Davis Cup Captain of the Indian team. It was an accidental meeting, just like tennis in my life.

I was the Davis Cup captain from 1993 to 1999 and used to visit Delhi very often in those days. It was during the Davis Cup preparation matches in the year 1994 that I, Leander and Mahesh were invited to dinner by a common friend to the Delhi Gymkhana Club. This was Micky Chatterjee, my very good school-time friend. We were supposed to meet elsewhere, but at the last minute, he had changed the venue.

When we reached the club, our host had not arrived yet. Over the phone, he told us to go to the bar and wait for him. When we went to the bar, we were suddenly accosted by a young, attractive and very well-dressed woman who came up and introduced herself. This was Sharmin. She was sitting at one of the tables with some friends who were tennis aficionados.

When we walked in, they recognised us and told her about India's Davis Cup team. At that time, she did not know anything about tennis or Davis Cup or anything connected with it. When they saw us, her friends told her to come up to us and ask us to join their table. Which she did very graciously. It all started there.

Actually, it was a rare chance meeting, as they say, something extraordinary happens when you least expect it. We hit it off right from the very start. I came to Delhi off and on in those years, and we met every time.

Sharmin Choudhury was born in east Pakistan, now Bangladesh. Her father, Professor Shirazul Islam Choudhury, was an educationist and philosopher. Her family was large and inclusive – like all Bengali families on both sides of the divide were until the turn of the century – and she said, a carnival was always going on at her home… especially at lunch, TV and dinner time as she grew up. From the 1970s, her large family had started to migrate to the USA and Europe. Sharmin had grown up and studied in Dhaka but her actual practical education came from the USA. Her mother, who had been visiting Bangladesh, died in 1989 in Dhaka. Her father died in Los Angeles in 1996. Those were tough years for her.

As far as I was concerned, Sharmin was the total package – she had all the qualities a man could ask for – a great homemaker and companion and a fantastic administrator. She also had a great sense of humour and loved life just as I did. A Bengali, she empathised with my Kolkata connections. In the next few years, I got to know Sharmin better. She had been married and had two young sons, Saif and Omar; their mother said, they were her biggest achievements. She was, literary, a working mother. In the USA, she had two-three Italian restaurants, which she had run for ten years. But her real interest was in the creative field.

Sharmin came to India with a vision and worked very hard, starting with fashion designing. She lived in San Francisco and her first Indian assignment was a fashion shoot for the Bank of America. I learnt that she did a lot of ramp shows in Delhi, her models used to be Susmita Sen, Shikha Swaroop, Queenie Singh, Anupama Dev, Mukul Dev and others. When I met her, she was also doing documentary films as a creative director for visuals such as *The Indian*, which was very successful.

She worked for *National Geographic* and *Discovery* channels. Sometimes, I would go and watch her shooting. She was also creating a musical greats' documentary.

Since she was not from India, Sharmin really did not know of the power of my achievements, my big name, its importance to the nation. We became just friends without any expectations. We were attracted to each other but I lived in Kolkata and she worked in Delhi, so it was an on-and-off affair, we would meet when I was in Delhi. As an afterthought, Sharmin has told a friend, 'I never thought of getting married to him. My friendship with Jai was very sweet. Jai is not an easy person to know, one has to dig deep to know him. He is simple, friendly but never discusses his pain or problems unless he knows that person very well. What attracted me to him is that he was a thorough gentleman. My fear at that time was that he was going to give space... he always does'.

As casual friends, we lost touch with each other several times over the next many months. I discovered the kindness in Sharmin when I came to Delhi for a knee operation. I had family back in Kolkata but no one had accompanied me for this odyssey. When I dropped in to see her, she was shocked that I had come alone from Kolkata. So, the next day, she came to the hospital to see me and nursed me till I left for Kolkata again, healed.

We became serious after this about our relationship. We were no longer dating casually. I knew in the late nineties that Sharmin was the one for me and I proposed to her and luckily, she accepted. We were married in 2001. We have been together for twenty-two years now. On hind sight, I feel that if I had met Sharmin fifteen years earlier, I would have been a more successful person. Saif and Omar, Sharmin's sons, are my sons now. They are more like friends; we discuss everything from sports to music and girls. Saif is a great guy and now lives in San Francisco and Omar lives in Austin, Texas. I have known Omar since he was eight and stayed with us until he went back to the USA when he was 16 for higher studies. I look forward to meeting them every time.

Omar, Jenni and little Sabine

Saif, with wife Sharmin and sons

Sharmin is a multi-faceted and multi-talented person. She is an innovative chef and curates miracle Mughlai meals – this to the amazement of my friends and visitors. For me, these days, it's most often just soup and what a delight even this is.

She is a Yoga guru and pushes me even now to do yoga and to go to the gym regularly, which I know I have to do for my own good. I am a lazy guy and we do not have house help. She is always telling me to go to the kitchen and tells me, *ei jao coffee ta banao* (make coffee). Being a creative person, she sometimes loses her cool and patience, but that's only for a short while, and more often rightly so.

Not only very creative, she is also very hard-working in whatever she does. When she first came to visit me in Kolkata, she changed my whole life completely with her creative perspective. I was building my home in Salt Lake at that time. She simply took over and made a great job of mapping the house with her ideas and interior designing experience. She is someone who, when she puts her mind to something she will do to the best of her ability.

Sharmin is the chairperson of the Jaidip Mukerjea Tennis Academy and runs the academy with an iron fist and singlehandedly. But she also has a very soft and compassionate touch with the staff, coaches and trainees. Our tennis academy in Kolkata is considered one of the best in the country and this is only due to Sharmin. You can say that the academy is her baby and her showpiece.

Sharmin was also very close to my friend Premjit Lall. When he was not well (1940-2008), we used to visit him very often. And on Prem's birthday on 20th of October, in his last years, Sharmin made it a point to visit him with a special cake and cigarettes, which Prem liked but was not allowed to smoke and appreciated the gesture. Sharmin has a heart of gold and goes out of her way to make these kind gestures, full of love.

There is a spiritual side to Sharmin that I soon discovered. She was born in a hardcore Muslim family, but she does not confine herself to just one religious' realm. She is not religious. She believes with her mind and soul in karma, discipline, prayers, humanity and to be down to earth because karma, she thinks, is the only thing that gives us Moksha.

Sometimes I shudder to think that had Sharmin not come into my life, what would have happened to me? Even now Sharmin looks after everything that is mine and forces me to play, exercise and really takes care of me. They say marriages are made in heaven, I am sure that ours was and I thank God for giving me such a special person as my life partner. She is my rock of Gibraltar.

My Jaidip Uncle

HAVING A NATIONAL HERO as a stepfather seems more fiction than reality because he never presented himself as an overtly revered figure.

The true heroic quality of Jaidip Mukerjea is that he is extremely approachable and kind. In fact, when I first met him as a ten-year-old, I had just started playing tennis and I asked him if he had ever played. 'A little bit,' he responded nonchalantly. He never shared his tennis exploits because I gather, he wanted me to like him for his personality.

After our first visit, my mother explained all that he had accomplished in his career, and I immediately had two thoughts. One, I couldn't believe this person was casually sitting in my

★ DAVIS CUP TRIUMPH: India's Premjit Lal smashes powerfully during the crucial doubles encounter against Japan in the Davis Cup Eastern Zone final at Tokyo. Lal and Mukherjea beat Toshiro Sakai and Jun Kamiwazumi, 7-9, 6-1, 3-5, 6-1, 8-6, and went on to win the tie, 3-2.

room, watching my tiny 23-inch Panasonic TV. And the second being, that I would need to improve my tennis game significantly before he would watch me play for the first time.

During that first year, we would watch tennis, cricket, football, even Sylvester Stallone movies together. As he was dating my Mom, I didn't know how to address him, so, I just called him, 'Jaidip Uncle,' a name that has stuck till today.

After my parents wed in 2001, he essentially became my guardian. He did the whole nine yards. He went to tennis matches (to mostly watch me lose), attended parent-teacher meetings, planned vacations. We shared some amazing memories together. He was always available and willing to discuss anything that was on my mind. He would never get offended or take things personally. He provided a new level of emotional consistency, which was a new experience for me.

Over the next years, I had a front row seat to bear witness to all of Jaidip Mukerjea's accomplishments and victories, both on and off the court. We celebrated wins, such as awards, career milestones and mourned losses. He would always explain to me that, 'You're going to lose more than you'll ever win,' which is true not just in tennis but life itself.

While this book is going to share a litany of impressive feats, to me his most heroic quality is being the perfect role model for a shy ten-year-old kid. I am thrilled that the rest of you can learn more about my Jaidip Uncle.

—**Omar Abdullah**

Chapter 11

FRIENDSHIPS ON AND OFF THE COURT

I HAVE HAD many friends, being a senior tennis player in the international circuit. Many of them have now passed away but among those who come to mind is first of all Premjit Lall. We travelled the world together but we had a funny relationship. We were rivals because we were number One and number Two players in the country but our support groups included each other. And Akhtar Ali.

Premjit Lall

Akhtar Ali

Ramanathan Krishnan

The most unlikely friend I have is Ramanathan Krishnan (b. 1937). He is from Tamil Nadu. He was a great tennis player but we had nothing in common. He was a typically South Indian guy – he stayed home, he didn't mix much, he didn't like movies or going to parties but he is a very honest person and he used to be full of advise; he never came to give you advice voluntarily but if you asked him, he would advise. Although I was three-four years younger, he was always very good to me. Talking to him was enlightening. We talked not just about tennis and sports; we shared jokes and talked about music, the Beatles and Rolling Stones and Urban Monk and others… many had performed in Calcutta.

One friend was Arthur Robert Ashe, the first Black American player in the international circuit, which had been dominated by white players before Ashe's advent. I used to hang out a lot with Arthur. Arthur (10 July 1943 - 6 February 1993) started playing as a six-year-old and won three Grand Slam Singles. The US Open main court is today named Arthur Ashe Court. He took me to several Afro-American concerts. He died young from an ailment.

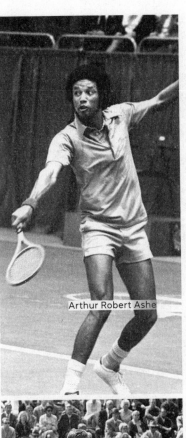

Arthur Robert Ashe

Another tennis friend who was very close to me in the same bracket as Tony Roche was Manuel Santana. He was a Wimbledon champion and we were very close, we used to travel a lot together, have dinner and then go to some great parties.

Tony Roche

The male circuit would play separately from the female circuit but I had some friends among the women players. There was Sandra Reynolds, a female player from South Africa. There

Manuel Santana

Margaret Court

was Margaret Court who I know quite well. She is Australian and was the World number 1. Recently I met her at Wimbledon. Margaret was a great player, probably even better than Serena.

An international friend is Alan Fox. He is a doctorate, a PhD. He was a great tennis player and we travelled a lot of the circuits together. He retired and became the tennis coach of a very good sports college in California, the Pepperdine College. He is one of the gurus of tennis and was a fantastic coach – mental coach and physical coach, both. He used to play at that level – it will be thought not fought. I do keep in touch with him. The last time I was in LA, I met him and we had lunch with him.

I was very friendly with several cricketers of yesteryear – Tiger Pataudi, the Nawab of Pataudi, M L Jaisimha, Abbas Ali Baig and Farookh Engineer. When we became friends, tennis and cricket were roaring in Kolkata.

The former prime minister of Bhutan, Lhendup Dorji, was a very close friend. I first met him in school and then in London where he was in exile. Often, we would play together so when he moved back to Bhutan, he invited me. Even now, his daughter is very close to Sharmin and we go off to Bhutan very often. Another friend in Bhutan is Benji Dorji, who was Chief Justice of Bhutan, we have had great times together.

Another guy I knew was Donald Dell. He was a sports attorney and used to play the circuits with us. He was a sports agent for the biggies (like IMG), and represented Arthur Ashe, Stan Smith, Jimmy Connors, and Ivan Lendl during the golden age of professional tennis (1975 to 1985). He was also the founder of Professional Services (ProServ), one of America's first sports marketing firms, established in 1970.

In the Australia circuit, I travelled a lot with Bob Carmicheal, Tony Roche, John Newcombe and Roger Taylor. We became very good friends and we are still in touch with each other, unfortunately Bob Carmicheal passed away a few years ago. In Chennai I had a very good friend called Johny

Prabhakar, he was a decent tennis player and played for Indian circuit. We kept our friendship and whenever I visited Chennai we would meet.

A good friend and a good player was (P) Chopra Sardarji. So was Dipu Banerjee from Allahabad, his father owned the A H Wheeler & Co which sold books at railway stations in India. I had another close friend, Suresh Sharma, someone I met in London. He studied architecture there. I haven't seen much of him in recent years.

Another person who I really miss is Pradip Bajoria, who unfortunately passed away a couple of years ago at the prime of his life. He, along with Rajit Pillai, were two of the more talented players in the South Club coaching scheme. Once Pradip reached the senior level, he realised that he was not going to make it as a professional tennis player, therefore he concentrated on business and did really well. He was a big contributor to Junior Tennis and sponsored a lot of players. I still can't believe Pradip is gone, what a fine gentleman! RIP Pradip.

Rajit Pillai, who now lives in Hyderabad, was also a very talented tennis player and played tournaments abroad. He learnt his tennis in South Club but has now stopped playing and concentrates on business and parties!

My father had a cousin called P L Roy but everyone knew him as Hurricane Roy. He was a great guy and I was very fond of him, I treated him more like a friend than an uncle. Whenever I went to play in Delhi, I used to stay with him. He worked for Metal Box and was posted in Delhi. He had a wonderful English wife whom I call aunty Jane and two sons named Tempest and Loo. Tempest is the now famous Prannoy Roy of NDTV fame.

Hurricane kaka's father, P L Roy senior, was the doyen of Indian boxing in the early 20th century and named his sons after storms. So, his first son was called Hurricane, the second son Typhoon and the third son Cyclone. Hurricane kaka called his two sons Tempest and Loo.

Later on, Hurricane kaka moved to London and I have spent some wonderful times with him in London.

I must relate a funny story here. He was having a party in his house in London and I was invited. I was a little clumsy and before the party, he warned me not to drop anything. As luck would have it, during the party a waiter by mistake bumped into me and his tray with drinks fell to the floor and made a huge noise. When Hurricane kaka heard the noise, he said loudly, 'it can only be Jaidip!!' I was so embarrassed but he went on, 'I knew it! I knew it!'

Anyway, this was soon forgotten and the party went on and on. Great times with a great uncle-friend. I don't see much of Tempest, but whenever we meet, we have a great time and talk about our earlier days.

I HAVE A lot of younger friends and acquaintances. There was a Calcutta boys' group. Chirodeep Mukerjea, my younger brother, was in this circle with Bidyut Goswami. Then there were Gaurav Misra, Murli Bhalotia (of Tolly Club) and a guy called Rana. Somdev Devvarman and Mahesh Bhupathi are very close. Somdev was a very good sportsperson, now he is a TV commentator. He is also a very good musician and has a band.

In tennis, you find a lot of people who start playing very early and don't continue their studies. Somdev studied at a university, in North Carolina and he won the very prestigious NCAA tournament which is the top tennis tournament for college students. The best player coming out of that system is John Isner, he is World number 2 or 3. I think that college education is very important in a man's life.

Though I am senior, the guy now close to me is Debal Banerjee, my cousin and son of the former Attorney General of India Milan Banerjee. I meet Debal the most now as he shuttles between Kolkata and Delhi. Our families were related so we know each other for ages, only now in the past few years have we become really close.

Rahul Basu, Nausher Madan, Pravin Singh are among other younger people who are friends. Rahul's father, Tutu Basu, was a good friend of my father and they used to play tennis together at South Club and party together. We carried on from there and became good friends.

Pravin now lives in New York. I met him first when he started playing tennis at South Club. He was a decent player and a very good coach; he tries to come to India every year and we meet whenever we can.

Nausher Madan was a very promising tennis player and left India on a Tennis scholarship for the U S and only came back once, but we meet whenever I am in the States. I am in constant touch with them on WhatsApp and reminisce about our good old days at the South Club and Kolkata of 1969-'70s. Debal, Rahul and I make it a point to be together at Wimbledon in the summer and Kolkata in the winters. We are all from the South Club and as my good friend Akhtar Ali would have said:

We are all South Club graduates.

In Kolkata among my friends are Murli Bhalotia, Vinoo Nath, Rupinder Singh and Anil Mukerji who is a good tennis player and former Managing member of the Tollygunge Club.

Tony and the Medicine Man

NOW, I WOULD like to share an interesting story, related to my dear friend Tony Roche, and his woes with a nagging tennis elbow. My friendship with Tony began in the early 1960s and still exists today. Even though we reside in our native countries Australia and India, which are separated by thousands of miles, the miles have never been a barrier to our friendship.

Tony, the man with a tough exterior and an extremely soft and sensitive interior, was a formidable force in the World Tennis Circuit of the 1960s. He was considered by many (including Harry Hopman and Rod Laver) to be the heir apparent of Australian Tennis, after Lew Hoad and Rod Laver, though he could win only one Grand Slam Singles Title, the French Open in 1966. His game and technique were of a different level.

Tony later proved his mettle by producing four World Champions – Ivan Lendl, Patrick Rafter, Roger Federer, Lleyton Hewitt – and numerous international players as a coach. In my opinion, Tony is one of the greatest coaches that World Tennis has ever produced. But his best years as a player were lost , due to a nagging tennis elbow. Even after consulting the best physicians and surgeons of Europe, America and Australia, he was not able to find a suitable cure.

Then strangely, Tony got a suggestion from a doctor friend in London, to visit a Faith Healer, residing in the mountains of Cebu City, Philippines. As a last resort, Tony decided to fly all the way from London to the Philippines. Upon reaching the dwelling of the Faith Healer, he and his wife were quite surprised to see a large crowd gathered for the Healer's healing touch.

After hearing out Tony's medical history, Tony was put in a trance or rather hypnotised, as the Healer performed a minor surgery on his arm. A small cut was made around Tony's elbow, and some indigenously prepared medicine was applied on to it. After wrapping the incision with a banana leaf, Tony was asked to leave. But with the warning not to bathe for two days and not play for a month.

As they say, facts are stranger than fiction. Tony's agonizing elbow was miraculously cured. But, by then, some of the best days of Tony as a player were already lost. If the injury had not happened to Tony, the History of Tennis, could have been a little different.

So, I would like to advise: train, practice and play hard but with precaution and evaluation. This shall prolong your sporting career.

This time when I went to Wimbledon, I met Tony and his wife and Roger and we had dinner together twice. He still plays tennis and he still keeps it up. Tony Roche is one of the best coaches in the world, he coached Federer. We are very close and we keep in touch on the phone. He was supposed to come to Kolkata for a visit before the pandemic but unfortunately, because of the pandemic there was a bereavement in his family, he lost his wife. Maybe, this winter I will persuade him to come to India.

Tony Roche on Jaidip Mukerjea

I HAVE KNOWN Jay for over 50 years and he has been a great friend over this time. Even though we did not play against each other that many times on tour, I had a huge respect for his game.

The one time we did play against each other was in the 1966 Davis Cup Challenge Round in Melbourne. He and Krish beat Newcombe and me in 4 sets, of which Jay always reminds me when we catch up. I have always had a huge respect for Indian tennis, especially in the 1960s. Jay was a huge part of

that history. I was so glad I never played in India during these times, as they had a great record playing at home.

I have enjoyed Jay's company, we got to know each other on the Caribbean tour in 1966. Jay was travelling with his good friend Premjit Lall and we had such good times together.

In recent times, I have travelled to Jay's academy in Calcutta and worked with some of the promising Indian players. I always look forward to these visits. During the last six years, I have had a very stressful and tough time on a personal note. Jay and Sharmin helped me so much during this time in which I will always be so grateful. Your friend always.

Rod Laver on JM

I FIRST MET Jay in 1961 at Wimbledon and later in 1962, when he, along with Premjit Lall, came for the Australian circuit. Both Prem and Jay got along very well with the Australian players and vice versa.

Jaidip was a very fine player, a gentleman and has won a few tournaments in the world circuit. Jay also had a great Davis Cup record and was one of the key players of the Indian team who took India to the Challenge round in 1966. Unfortunately, I couldn't play for Australia at that time as I had already turned pro.

Jay was also a good Squash player; we used to play a lot of squash during his trip to Australia in 1962. I wish him all the very best with the book he is writing and I am sure it will be a great read.

Jaidip (right) with Rod Laver (left) and Ray Moore, Tournament Director,
Indian Wells tournament.

Allen Fox on JM

BACK IN THE 1960s, when I was playing the tour, the game was beautiful and fun because the players were all friends and close. We called it 'the circuit' because we tended to play clusters of tournaments in the same area, keeping travel costs down, and also because the various 'circuits' tended to follow the weather. So, there was a January circuit in Australia, a spring circuit in the Caribbean, and summer circuits in the United States and Europe.

We got close as players because we practiced together, stayed at the same hotels, ate meals together, travelled together (often by car), and competed against each other. We were amateurs, but nevertheless we were paid 'appearance' money by the various tournaments. This differed in amount depending on the tournament record, rankings, reputation, and public recognition of the individual player.

The best players in the world in those days – Roy Emerson, Rod Laver, Manuel Santana – were paid about $1,000 a week. The next level – Stolle, Roche, Newcombe, Ralston (and I'm guessing) – $500- $800. Jay and I were probably at a similar level, and I got between $200 - $400. We could beat the top guys sometimes and had some name recognition, but we did not win the major tournaments like Wimbledon, the French, the US, or Australian (obviously).

Jay and I had been bumping into each other for years on the tour, but got even closer when we were playing a couple of Spring tournaments in Scandinavia – Stockholm and Helsinki. The first was Helsinki and it was icy cold. Of course, we warmed up playing, but otherwise around the courts we warmed up standing as close as we dared to a 50-gallon steel drum filled with flaming debris of some kind (not quite the plush tournament environment of today). As I recall, Jay and I met in the finals, and Jay beat me in a tight, three-set match where I actually held a match point.

The tour, back in the day, differed from today's tour in

multiple ways besides just money and keeping warm with barrels of incendiaries. One other aspect of the tour occurred because we were often called upon to make our own calls. Since we were all friends and concerned about being fair to each other, we were especially scrupulous about these calls. But we often had umpires. A tricky situation sometimes occurred with umpires, when our opponent got a bad call. Should we over-rule the umpire or not; or maybe we should throw the next point.

My normal approach was to talk to my opponent before the match and say, 'Look, if you get a bad call feel free to squawk about it as much as you like. If I get one, I will squawk. But let's not throw points or intercede if the other guy gets a bad call'. My idea was to keep from being a bad guy when my opponent got a bad call and yet be able to complain as I wished, when I got one.

As fate would have it, Jay and I met in the Final in Stockholm also. Early in the match, I got a bad call. Jay, sportsman that he is and despite our agreement not to do this, threw the next point anyway.

Another close match. At a crucial point, deep in the third set, Jay got a bad call. I needed that point and I wanted to win the title, so the thought entered my mind about NOT throwing the next point. I felt that if I took that point, I would win the match and title, but lose my friendship with Jay. So, I threw the point. And because of it, I am now writing this recollection of my time with my dear friend, Jay, without regret. He beat me in the Helsinki final, and I beat him in the finals at Stockholm.

As it should be.

Mahesh Bhupathi on JM

WHEN I WAS INVITED to Join the Indian Davis cup Team in Jaipur in September 1994 for India's tie against South Africa, I was still in college at the University of Mississippi.

Clearly, it was going to be both one of the most exciting and nerve wracking experiences of my yet-to-start professional career at that point. It was also the beginning of my amazing friendship with Sir Jadip. He was many things to Indian tennis. An Indian Tennis Icon, our Davis Cup Captain but what very few people knew about him was that he was always one of the boys.

The team at that time had a lot of senior players but he always went out of his way at every session or every meal or even every time he saw me at the hotel to check in on me, give me comfort, make sure I was taking the experience in and not putting too much pressure on myself.

Over the better part of the next twenty-five years, there has rarely been a big match I played when Sir Jaidip hasn't wished me, consoled me or celebrated with me, albeit virtually. One of the things I used to look forward to every year was to look up, during my first round match at Wimbledon and seeing Sir Jaidip in the stands rooting for us. It has been customary for him to attend the championships every year and that tradition is a special one.

The relationship we have developed is also a special one. Sir Jaidip has given back to Indian tennis in many ways including his amazing tennis academy in Kolkata and I will always be on his team and wish him the best on his journey to pen down his memoirs.

Ramesh Krishnan on JM

JAI HAS THE unique Indian record of reaching the last 16 in the singles of the four 'majors'. What is worth mentioning is that he reached the fourth round at Wimbledon on four different occasions and has been a bit unlucky not to have made it past that round even once.

Jaidip's game was built around a good forehand and a strong pair of legs. When we met in 2020, he told me that he still makes it a point to make sure he keeps his legs in good working condition. His playing style was a bit unorthodox and that broke the rhythm of his opponents. And of course, he was a very courageous player. He could play well under pressure. And this is borne out by his excellent Davis Cup record.

He was the mainstay of the Indian Davis Cup team for most of the 1960s and the early 70s.

The highlight of course was India making the Challenge Round in 1966. He scored an important win against Wilhem

Bungert of Germany and was an important part of doubles victories both against Brazil and the famous win over the top doubles team in the world, John Newcombe and Tony Roche in the 1966 Challenge Round.

It is my regret that our paths did not cross more often on the tennis courts. By the time I was ready to play the senior tournaments in India, he had cut back on his appearances and the few tournaments that we did participate in, we did not get to face each other. And much later, he took over as the Indian Davis Cup team captain just after I retired from the team.

I am very happy that Jai has used his time during this pandemic to put down his thoughts and I am sure he will have plenty to say about a period when India was one of the top tennis playing nations. I will read it with great interest.

Somdev Devvarman on JM

FOR AN ATHLETE, accomplishments are everything. But what comes after you're done with accomplishments? What happens when someday you meet the players of the next generation? How will they look at the legacy you have left? What kind of relationship will you have with your peers from different eras? What is that, which is beyond mere accomplishments?

Growing up in Calcutta and being connected to tennis, Jaidip Mukerjea was a household name. But our paths never

crossed while I lived there. After all, I was just eight years old when my family moved to Chennai. To be honest, I had heard of how good the tennis tradition in Calcutta was back in the day. Of the historic South Club, the Davis Cup matches in the Wimbledon of the East, and of the many great players who hailed from the city. But the two names on the very top were always Jaidip Mukerjea and Premjit Lall. So, there it began. A next genner's connection with a legend of the game.

The first time I got to spend a little time with Jai (as I fondly call him now) was in Feb 2004. I was given a wild card to play the Futures Tournament being conducted at the Saturday Club where Jai was the tournament director. Being a wild card entrant, I was coming in with zero expectations. All I really wanted to do was not embarrass myself and prove that the wild card was justified.

For some odd reason, Jaidip seemed to have a different train of thought. After an average performance in my first round, a gritty but certainly not a pretty tennis match (which I ended up winning), I was a little rattled as I was stretching after the match. I remember Jai walking up to me very excited about the win and telling me how much fun he had watching me.

I said, 'Really? Are you sure you're not mixing me up with the Thai guy who played next to me?'

He laughed and replied, 'I enjoyed it because it's not often you see an Indian tennis player with strong legs. You've got strong legs, and a fighter's mentality. Keep this up and you can go places'.

Hmmmm, I thought. 'Are we talking about the same

person here? Jai had watched the match, and didn't harp on everything I did badly, but instead came and complimented me on my personality and my strength. I must be missing something.'

The next thing I remember is lifting the trophy. My conversations with Jai over the course of that week had somehow helped me find some inner belief that I didn't even know existed. It was the first Futures title of my life.

Meetings with Jai became a little more frequent, once I made it to the Davis Cup squad in 2008.

That's when our relationship started to grow. I remember one of the first times we were hanging out, and I asked him if he wanted me to call him Sir or Jai. He laughed and said, 'You can call me Jai. How does it matter? Half the people who are called Sir in this world are made fun of behind their backs anyway!' Jai was different and he always intrigued me.

Sure, his accomplishments were top notch. But there was something else there. An aura of sorts. An energy about him. He was fun loving, big hearted and he was always one of the boys. We were there for one another. Keep in mind, I'm talking about developing a friendship with someone who was born forty-three years before me!

In 2014, I lost a tight 5-setter in the first round of Wimbledon to Jerzy Janowicz. Jai and Sharmin Aunty sat and watched the whole thing. Obviously dejected and sitting and with my girlfriend (now wife) Shivali, I got a call from Jai in the evening. He said, 'Som great match, if you're up for it, come join us at a pub in Earl's court'. Shivali heard the call, looked

Sania, Somdev and Amritraj

at my face and said, 'Let's go. This'll be so much fun!' And fun it was! Jai just always has a way of saying the right thing at the right time. And at that time, all I needed was a drink with my friends. When it was time to relax and enjoy ourselves, that's what we did.

And when it was time to train, Jai called his old friend, Tony Roche and organised a camp for the Indian boys to come and learn. Think of the opportunity for us – to spend time with someone who has won a singles Grand Slam along with 15 doubles and has also coached greats of the games like Lleyton Hewitt, Pat Rafter and Roger Federer. He was now in Calcutta to train a bunch of Indian players! All because Jaidip Mukerjea picked up the phone and invited his friend over.

Among his many admirable qualities, this is the one that has always stood out for me. The quality of friendship that comes along with Jaidip Mukerjea. Not just Tony Roche, but almost anyone he's spent time with is willing to oblige when Jai asks. As simple as that.

My time with Tony Roche was special but I don't know if I cherish the time on court more or the dinners where he and Jai would discuss stories from the old days.

We would all ask question after question. Undoubtedly a pretty great package for all of us. The foundations of this friendship were laid before any of us were born. If it sounds surreal, it's because it was.

As I mentioned earlier, the name Jaidip Mukerjea was always linked with the name Premjit Lall – the two handsome tennis players from Calcutta, who travelled the world and played at the highest level of the game. But more importantly to me, they were 'best friends'. Given the state of Indian tennis I grew up in, 'best friends on the circuit' sounded incredibly special.

I never had the honour of meeting the man, but when Jai decided to host the Premjit Lall memorial tournament a few years ago, the whole Indian tennis circuit was incredibly touched by the gesture. In typical fashion, with just one phone call from Jai everybody showed up.

From the outside it might have looked like a small event. After all Jai had organised all big tennis events in Calcutta, including the WTA and different exhibitions with greats such as Martina Navratilova present. Jai even managed to make 'Didi' hit tennis balls with Sania!

This event, just like all the others, had the special Jaidip touch. It was about bringing the tennis community together and doing what's best for the game while remembering Premjit Lall and what their friendship stood for.

Every year they did the event, he and Sharmin Aunty would

do it in style. They ensured that every player invited had a blast during the week – play tennis, mingle with their contemporaries and leave with memories and friendships. Something simple yet important that all of us, the younger generation, needs to learn and carry forward.

What is that, which is beyond mere accomplishments? As I ask myself this question, I need to look no further than Jaidip Mukerjea. A legend for more reasons than one. A great friend to many.

The importance of good people: Imran Mirza

THE IMPORTANCE OF good people in our lives is just like the importance of heartbeats. It is not visible but silently supports our life. Jaidip Mukerjea is one such very important person in my life.

In the last half a century that I have known Jaidip, we have come a long way. I was a little boy many years ago, when my Dad took me to watch a tennis match on the grass courts of New Delhi where a couple of handsome Indian tennis players, Jaidip Mukerjea and Premjit Lall, were playing against the Romanian superstars, Ilie Nastase and Ion Tiriac. It was the Indian duo that captured my imagination on that fateful day and, perhaps, the seeds were sown for my love for the game that culminated in the emergence of Sania Mirza as a tennis player on the world stage three decades later.

Jaidip Mukerjea hails from a highly respected family of Bengal. He is the great-grandson of revered Indian freedom fighter, Chittaranjan Das and his maternal uncle was the former

Chief Minister of Bengal, Siddhartha Shankar Ray. Despite his political affiliations, Jaidip's passion for tennis superseded all other interests and it was in this sport that he was destined to earn fame for his country.

While I watched Jaidip on the tennis courts with awe and pride every time he won on the international stage or represented India in the Davis Cup in which he had some amazing results, it was in 2005 after Sania had made her international breakthrough, that I got an opportunity to

Imran Mirza

meet Jai at a personal level. We immediately struck a chord of empathy and I found his genial, affable demeanour extremely loveable. It was Jaidip who arranged a coaching stint for Sania with his great friend, Tony Roche at a time when the Australian superstar was working with Roger Federer and this provided an opportunity for me, as well, to imbibe several intricacies of the game from the great man, that has added to my own knowledge and exposure to tennis.

Jaidip Mukerjea's heroics on the tennis courts are well-known and part of sporting folklore but his doubles win with Krishnan as partner in the 1966 Davis Cup final against Australia over John Newcombe and Tony Roche will be remembered for a long time. His record of having reached the last-16 stage in singles in each of the four Grand Slams speaks volumes of Jaidip's proficiency on all surfaces. He is a 3-time Asian Champion and some of his other noteworthy achievements included wins over the likes of Roy Emerson, Fred Stolle, Arthur Ashe and Manuel Santana. In his early years, as a Junior, Jaidip was the runner-up in the Wimbledon Boys Singles Championship 1960.

For well over a dozen years, Jaidip Mukerjea held centre stage of Indian tennis with his contemporaries, Ramanathan Krishnan and Premjit Lall and together, the trio was responsible for setting a solid foundation and a benchmark for the game in our country. After his retirement from the game, Jaidip continued to serve tennis in India. He was appointed the captain of the Indian Davis Cup team and then with help from his wife, Sharmin, he set up the Jaidip Mukerjea Tennis Academy that has nurturing talented players of India for several years now.

My visits to the 'City of Joy' over the last several years have now become synonymous for me with the man I admired even as a young boy and who inspired me to produce a women's tennis champion from our country. He is a very dear friend whose comradeship I value immensely. This autobiography of Jaidip Mukerjea is certain to not only provide a glimpse of the life and struggles of one of the superstars of Indian sports but will give a documented account of the development of the game in our country over several decades. A 'Collector's item' and a must-read for every lover of sport.

The Bhutan Connection

I FIRST MET LENNY DORJI (Lhendup Dorji), the dashing Bhutanese ex-prime minister, way back in Kolkata in 1960. He used to date Glenda, a daughter of one of the teachers in La Martiniere, Kolkata where I did my schooling. In the mid 1960s, when I was playing international tennis, Lenny was living in London and that's where we became very good friends. I use to take him to Wimbledon where he met some of my close tennis friends like Manuel Santana, Tony Roche, John Newcombe and others. He was the toast of Mayfair, with his debonair looks and made us members of almost every night club in London like the Saddle Room, Tramps etc. I really enjoyed his company, we all looked forward to meet him when the tennis circuit came to the UK.

Lenny, later opened the casino in Nepal and finally went back to Bhutan.

He was a sports man – a horse racing magnet and a very loyal friend. I was invited to Bhutan quite regularly and always had a great time fishing, hunting and playing tennis. On one occasion, we played an exhibition match in front of a full house. Lenny partnered His Majesty, the Fourth King of Bhutan and I partnered Lenny's nephew Benji Dorji. It was a close match and Benji and I won, much to the disappointment of the huge crowd. He also gifted me a Toyota car, which I used in Kolkata long before imported cars were allowed into India.

Lenny passed away a few years ago, but his legacy lives on, his daughter Khendum and my wife Sharmin are very close friends.

Khendum Dorji on JM

With friends from Bhutan.

I FIRST MET Jaidip Mukerjea as a child, in the 1970s in Bhutan. I had heard of this tennis legend who was a friend of my father, and had been to school in Calcutta at the same time as my mother.

I had heard stories of Wimbledon visits and partying in London with my parents, but I only met him in Thimphu when he came to play tennis with my father.

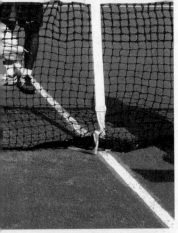

They were privileged to play a few tennis matches with His Majesty the Fourth King of Bhutan. Jaidip was still in great form and impressed all the local tennis enthusiasts. I found him to be a charming, down to earth and a sharp man who liked his whisky in the evenings. We met again several times in Calcutta at my father's Tivoli Court flat.

We only became friends though, many years later when he

Khendum and Jaidip.

visited Bhutan with his lovely wife, Sharmin. It was 2001 and Sharmin had given Jai a trip to Bhutan as a birthday gift. I arrived at the Taj one evening to take them out to dinner and met a gorgeous, grouchy lady who was now his wife. Sharmin was in a bad mood because she wasn't sure she wanted to meet me and, or have her second honeymoon interrupted. However, a few hours (and a bottle of Grey Goose) later, we realised we were soulmates and it was the start of a special friendship.

Since then, I have attended two of the Premjit Lall Invitational Tennis Tournaments at their academy. This is a wonderful initiative by Jaidip to remember and honour his late friend. I attended the matches daily and watched India's top young tennis players compete. They were all hardworking, sincere athletes with a great respect for Jaidip. I had the privilege to meet the Chief Minister of West Bengal, Mamata Banerjee, and also enjoyed making the acquaintance of Martina Navratilova, Mahesh Bhupathi, Sania Mirza and Vijay Amritraj.

Charu Sharma MCed both events and I thought he was one of the nicest men I've met. In 2015, Jaidip and Sharmin arranged an India-Bhutan Friendship Tournament in Thimphu in collaboration with the Bhutan Tennis Federation and the Indian Embassy, which was a great success. I would like to wish this enterprising and the charming couple all the best in all that they do.

We had a wonderful holiday together in Thailand a few years ago and often meet in Calcutta. Tashi Delek and I look forward to many more adventures together.

R Gopalakrishnan (Director Tata Sons) on JM

IT IS MY PLEASURE and honour to write a few words for Jaidip Mukerjea's book.

Pleasure, because I have known Jaidip for long years, though there were gaps in time. I first saw Jaidip in the 1950s, when quite literally, both of us were in our shorts!

Honour, because, in writing, I am joining great international tennis stalwarts, players whom I have grown up admiring!

Jaidip is four years older than I am. I joined the Bengal Lawn Tennis Association's Coaching Camp in South Club, Calcutta, around 1958. Jaidip had joined a few years earlier, along with Premjit Lall. Jaidip's competence and meteoric rise as a tennis player were inspirational as he went on to play for India in the Davis Cup and to win several international accolades.

Sometime in the 1960s, as Premjit and Jaidip were being felicitated at a function at the Willingdon Club, Bombay, they found themselves sitting next to a Parsi lady. In the polite chat that followed, the lady learnt that both upcoming youngsters would probably reduce their focus on their promising tennis careers to get a company job and earn a living. 'Oh, that would be a pity,' she had exclaimed. Sometime later, Premjit was offered a job at ACC Limited and Jaidip was offered a job at TISCO, both Tata companies. Thus, they could continue playing international tennis, bringing great laurels to India. The Parsi lady was Rodaben Sawhney, the sister of JRD Tata and the wife of Tata Director, Col Leslie Sawhney. Of such serendipity is life made!

Thirty-five years later, in 2002, when I was a Director of Tata, the group sponsored the Tata Open Tennis Tournament. Tata officers had invited the son of my college friend, Vece Paes, to attend the function. Leander Paes spoke feelingly about how he nearly abandoned the invitation to play international tennis in the early 1990s because the cost of a plane ticket was prohibitive – until TISCO agreed to pay for his journey abroad to play in a foreign tournament.

Jaidip has not only been an inspirational player, but also a great teacher through his JMTA – the Jaidip Mukerjea Tennis Academy at Calcutta. He has taken from the game but has also given back to the game.

I am sure his story will be an inspirational read for every reader of his book.

Habi and Moonmoon

BHARAT DEV BURMAN (also called Dev Varma) and his wife Moonmoon Sen, the actor, have been very good friends. In fact, Bharat, known popularly as Habi, is one of my oldest friends; his mother was the Princess of the Bengal state of Cooch Behar in the eastern foothills of the Himalayas. She married into one of the royal families of Tripura. Habi's mother died very young.

Bharat, or Habi, was brought up by the old Maharani of Cooch Behar, Indira Devi. Habi also happens to be the nephew of Maharani Gayatri Devi of Jaipur. As my aunt Swarupa Das (Buchi) was very close to the Cooch Behar family, whenever Bharat came to Kolkata, there was a big party for him. At that time, most winters he spent in Kolkata. Habi is married to the film star Moonmoon Sen, the daughter of the legendary Bengali actor Suchitra Sen. He has two daughters, both actors, Raima Sen and Riya Sen.

He was a very keen and avid golfer and has won some club tournaments in Kolkata. Even now, we get together quite frequently. Habi and I have spent many evenings together and we used to hang out in Park Street in the 1960s. What I enjoy about Habi is his sense of humour, knowledge of sports, and he is one of the best hosts when we are invited to dinner at his residence. In fact, the other day I had dinner with him. We are very very good friends.

Bharat Devvarma on JM

JAIDIP AND I GO a long way and now perhaps we are one of the few people who have memories of Calcutta's Golden Age. Although we don't meet often because of his hectic schedule and my mundane life (since retirement), we bond well whenever we meet.

I first remember Jai when my grandmother, the Maharani of Cooch Behar, held a birthday party for me in Calcutta

– when we were in our early teens. We had heard from his family that Jaidip wasn't keen on studies and slyly bunked classes to play tennis. His parents and aunt were close friends of my grandmother and her son, Bhaiya, the Maharaja of Cooch Behar. His great grandfather, the legendary C R Das's brother, S R Das, had founded one of the best education institutions in the country (the Doon School), based on the lines of Harrow and Eton.

Jai never spoke about his famous lineage nor of his achievements as an outstanding tennis player. I watched him win against Ramanathan Krishnan, who was considered one of the topmost World-level players at that time. Jai became a tennis star at a very early age. I used to follow Jai and company avidly. With Premjit, Jai won the Doubles partnership at Wimbledon.

Later when I started working in Calcutta, we began partying a lot together. Jai was fun, a great Rock-and Roller, which I envied.

He also had a streak of temper and once broke some tables and chairs at the restaurant called Blue Fox and once punched some guy at the CCFC Sports Club. Once, when we met in London, he tricked me into letting him use my membership at the exclusive Saddle Room Club. With his companions, on that occasion, Jai polished off all my stock of scotch reserved for me. Jai had briefly worked for the Tata Sons and I suspect that the sponsors fancied him.

My impression of Jai is that of an unassuming shy person, hot headed, a great talent plus a gentleman.

Moonmoon Sen on JM

JAI WAS ONE of those Bengalis, a tennis star, who wore a halo of fame very inconspicuously and with a shy smile.

I once begged him for a lesson because Vijay Amritraj was insisting that I play tennis for him in an exhibition match 'Sports Stars vs Film Stars' event sponsored by the ITC (I think).

With no idea of how to hold a racquet, I still could not help but notice how graceful Jai was in showing me how to swing my racquet. I, of course, thought that with his left arm around me, he was making a pass at me.

I first heard of him from my mother Suchitra who spoke of Jai and Premjit, while shooting for the film, *Saptapadi*. I then went on to meet his family, the dearest one was Bucchi Mashi, a close friend of the Cooch Behar family – that is Maa, Indira Devi, Bhaia Jagadipendra Narayan, Ayesha M, Gayatri Devi not to forget the nephews Bheem and Habi. What wonderful anecdotes of tiger shoots, food and fun they have. Jai has always been a favourite with my husband and I. Most Calcuttans know him as a South Club guy, always smiling, funny and smutty but so humble, never bragging about his games and achievements.

We always had a laugh whenever we met him at my husband's parties, on his birthday at the Royal and always will.

Chapter 12

—◆—

TRUE TO THE
MAHATMA'S WORDS

MOST OFTEN, GIVING back to the world remains a
dream for most people. My dream of giving back to the world,
however, is bearing fruit.

The International Tennis Federation (ITF) felicitated me
for my contribution to the game of tennis by awarding me the
Lifetime Achievement Award in 2003. I was the first Indian
to receive this world recognition. In 2021, Vijay Amritraj was
awarded a similar award.

I took from the world of tennis. I travelled the world for
tennis, met great players, heard great music, partied at great
places. Now, I wanted to give back something to the world, and
to my beloved Kolkata. What could it be?

Opportunity knocked at my door in 1999. In the 1990s,
as the Davis Cup captain, I used to go to Delhi very often, as
I have told you before. In one of the flights back to Kolkata,
the chief minister of West Bengal, Jyoti Basu was also was

travelling. As I knew him quite well, I went up to speak to him. After the usual chit chat, he suddenly asked me why I did not I open a tennis academy in Calcutta?

To this question, I had replied that, 'if you can sanction a piece of land, then surely, I will open a Tennis Academy in Salt Lake,' and that's how it all started.

Soon, Ashok Bhattacharya, the State's Urban Affairs minister, helped me to identify the land in FE block, Sec 3 Salt Lake. This is how the Jaidip Mukerjea Tennis Academy started in March 1999.

Today it is a star institution; it brings the world of tennis and the who-is-who of all the circuits to India, at one place, for India's young tennis players. We have coached over 8,000 trainees in the age group 3-16 years so far. Some of our trainees have represented India and various States, some have got Tennis Scholarships in Universities abroad and some have become coaches and are working in different academies.

Apart from coaching we have organised 17 ITF (International Federation Tennis tournaments), both for men and women.

We have also organised coaching camps for the Indian Davis Cup Team (twice) under the guidance of world-famous Australian player and coach Tony Roche, who at that time was coaching none other than the great Roger Federer.

For the last seven years, we have also been organising the Premjit Lall Memorial Tournament. Most of the top Indian players play this event to pay homage to the tennis legend who passed away fourteen years ago.

At the academy, every year we have a famous tennis player as a mentor; in the past, players like Tony Roche, Vijay Amritraj, Mahesh Bhupathi, Sania Mirza and Somdev Devvarman have been the mentors. One thing I can say proudly – that our Tennis Academy in East India is the best. And according to Tony Roche, our clay courts compare with the Red Clay Courts of Roland Garros in Paris, where the French Open takes place.

The ambiance, the greenery and the serene atmosphere makes it a wonderful place to be in. All this would have not been possible without my wife Sharmin, who is the person responsible for all this.

Sharmin is the person behind the academy. Without her support and positive attitude, the academy would not have existed. I am really proud of her – when she came into my life everything changed for the better for me.

If anything, tennis has made me very confident and I didn't let the fame get to my head. One gets to be around celebrities and stars, but I am very confident and a sane person and honest. And as the Mahatma had blessed me at the beginning of my life, I have tried to remain true to his word – while I have played for my nation, been great, I have tried to remain good.

Chapter 13

OH! MY BELOVED CALCUTTA!

HOW I LOVE my Calcutta! The transition from CALCUTTA to KOLKATA has not been smooth and has come with a sense of great loss! The loss of ambience, the loss of glamour and glitz, the loss of a comfort zone. It's a loss I cannot define but I do feel. When I grew up in Calcutta, now Kolkata, it was one of the best cities to live in, it had everything.

Despite the Partition of Bengal, in the 1950s and 1960s, as people there were no differences between Hindus, Muslims, Sikhs and Christians, and we were all friends and respected each other's faiths and religions and lived in harmony. Calcutta was a city which had everything you could think of. The best of education, the best of sports, the best of music, culture, art and theatre.

It had the best schools and colleges – for school you had La'Martiniere, St Xaviers, Loreto House and many others and for colleges we had the famous Presidency College, St Xaviers College and Scottish Church College and Loreto and Bethun College.

Calcutta was also known as the sports capital of India and has produced many illustrious sports stars in yesteryear. Football is the most popular sports in Bengal and has produced many fine footballers such as Chuni Goswami, P K Banerjee, Shyam Thapa and many others. The three big football clubs were Mohun Bagan, East Bengal and Mohammedan Sporting Club who had fantastic supporters. I remember in the 1st division football league matches in the Maidan, the ground was always full of spectators and it was a treat to go and watch these matches.

Even hockey used to draw huge crowds and in the Beighton Cup hockey tournament, teams from all over India used to participate and we all eagerly looked forward to this tournament. To hockey, this city gave Olympians such as Leslie Cladius, Keshav Dutt and V Paes.

In tennis, Calcutta has produced many players such as Sumant Misra, Dilip Bose, Naresh Kumar, Akhtar Ali, Premjit Lall, Jaidip Mukerjea, Gaurav Misra, Chirodip Mukerjea and many others including Leander Paes who all have brought laurels to the city. In cricket, the city has contributed many players such as Pankaj Roy, P Sen, Amber Roy and Chuni Goswami who had the honour of captaining India in football and Bengal in Cricket. Those days, this city had the best tennis courts in Asia.

In the theatre, film and musical world Calcutta has produced many legendary persons such as Satyajit Ray, Mrinal Sen, Hrishikesh Mukherjee, Uttam Kumar, Soumitra Chatterjee, Suchitra Sen and others and in music Salil Chowdhury, Manna

Dey, Hemanto Mukhopadhay, Sachin Dev Burman, Rahul Dev Burman, Kishore Kumar and others. Here lived and worked poets like Tagore, Kazi Nazrul, Jibananado, writers like Sarat Chandra, artists like Jamini Roy and Ganesh Pyne and Calcutta was a centre of music and culture.

Before the advent of multiplexes, the city also boasted of some of the best cinema halls such as Light House, Metro, New Empire, Globe, Elite, Minerva and the famous Star theatre. Some of these cinema halls had bands to play music after the night shows, and people could enjoy themselves dancing and partying.

In the X-Mass season anyone worth his salt had to be in Calcutta as this was the time when Calcutta was at its very best. Beautiful weather, test cricket at Eden Gardens, international tennis at the South Club, horse racing and international Polo tournaments at the race course and the Polo grounds; the atmosphere was truly amazing. Sometimes, when I meet some old timers in Delhi and Mumbai they still talk about the good old days of Calcutta.

The City never sleeps! Not then, not now.

In the 1950s and '60s, all the major airlines flew through Calcutta, such as PanAm, British Airways, Cathay Pacific, Quantas, KLM, Air France, Japan Airlines and of course Air India and Indian Airlines. There is some reason why the British made their headquarters in Calcutta until 1912. The reason was that Calcutta was well connected with the Coal belt, Jute mills, tea gardens, steel mills and the small-scale industries in Howrah and Calcutta; I feel this is why large mercantile firms like Andrew Yule, Bird and Company, Balmer & Lawrie, James Finlay, Mackinnon & Mackenzie and Macneil & Barry setup their head offices in Kolkata. We also had the famous New Market and as the saying goes, you can get anything or order anything from this market even now it is the best place to shop.

A mini Broadway, the famous Park Street is known all over the world and it is Calcutta's sunset strip. Within about 200 meters of Park Street, we had so many restaurants, bars and night clubs. Starting from one side of the street you had the Chinese restaurant Peiping, Trincas, Kwality, Olypub, Moulin Rouge, Bar-B-Q, Blue Fox, Mocambo and the iconic eating place Sky Room. On the other side we had Waldorf, Flury's, Mags (Magnolia) and in the Russel Street corner we had India's hobby centre, owned by tennis legend Naresh Kumar. In Middleton Row, off Park Street we had Peter Cat and El Morocco and in Free School Street we had the famous Isaia's bar which catered mainly for shippies (sailors).

At that time, a lot of ships used to dock at Calcutta Port. It was a fantastic place to be in and whenever I was in Kolkata, in between playing all over the world, I used to meet my friends regularly at Trincas at tea time which had tea-time music. My friends in crime were Rahul Dasgupta, Gopal Rana, Shanks Dasgupta, Mahesh Malhotra, Ravi Singh, Ronny Lynch, Murli Balotia and Dilip Dey. We used to plan our evening from Trincas and then start our pub crawling. Unfortunately, Murli, Dilip, Ravi and I are the only ones alive to tell the tale of our heady and brilliant days on Park Street.

Our evening would start from Trincas and then go on to

Blue Fox and other places and finally finish of in the club called Golden Slipper, which was opposite of the Nizam's restaurant and the original place for 'kathi rolls'. Even now, Park Street in Kolkata is all decked up for Christmas and New Year and has a carnival atmosphere where everyone goes to enjoy BURRA DIN and New Years. This is only because of our Didi, Chief Minister Mamata Banerjee, who has decided to hold on to the spirit of Calcutta in today's Kolkata.

Calcutta is the only city in India which has a fantastic club culture. Some of the clubs are The Bengal Club, Calcutta Club, Tollygunge Club, RCGC, CC&FC, Swimming Club, Saturday Club, Calcutta South Club, Calcutta Swimming Club, Outram Club, Swiss Club which is now known as the International Club and Dalhousie Institute which is now known as DI. We also have clubs in the Maidan which cater to food and beverages such as Mohun Bagan Club, East Bengal Club, Calcutta Police Club, Customs Club, Dalhousie Athletic Club, Rangers Club and The Parsee Club. So, you can guess how much the people of Kolkata-Calcutta know how to really enjoy themselves.

Calcutta also had two top hotels which had night clubs and cabarets. The Grand Hotel owned by the Oberois had a night club called Princess and an outdoor restaurant cum music podium called Shehrazade. The Princess had a live band with dancers from abroad and the Shehrazade had live music with a dance floor which catered mainly to the younger crowd. The Great Eastern Hotel, made famous in literature, was owned by the Billimorias. It had two famous restaurants and they were called Sherry's and Maxim's. Maxim's was the night club with a live band and foreign cabaret dancers and Sherry's was a bar-cum-restaurant. As a young man growing up in Calcutta I had the best time of my life in the golden days of Calcutta in the sixties and seventies.

For me Calcutta is still Calcutta and not yet Kolkata!

JAIDIP'S SECRETS

Favourite Sports: (other than Tennis) Golf

Sports person who inspired me: Bobby Riggs (Tennis); Mohammed Ali (Boxing)

Favourite Tennis Venue: Wimbledon

Toughest opponents: Roy Emerson; Ramanathan Krishnan

Memorable Victory (Singles): Wilhelm Bungert from Germany in Davis Cup at New Delhi

Memorable Victory (Doubles): Partnering Ramanathan Krishnan to beat the Australian Pair of John Newcombe & Tony Roche in Melbourne

Toughest Match: Wilhelm Bungert of Germany in Davis Cup Semifinal in Delhi

Memorable Davis Cup Ties: Ties against West Germany (New Delhi), Brazil (Kolkata) & Australia (Melbourne) in 1966

Important Victories: Roy Emerson, Quebec City; Ramanathan Krishnan, Kolkata; Roger Taylor, Wimbledon; Fred Stolle, Beckenham

Favourite Destination: London

Favourite Food: Italian food

Favourite Drink: Fresh Lime

Favourite Drink: Scotch

Favourite Singers: Mohammad Rafi, Frank Sinatra, Dean Martin

Favourite Song: *Strangers in the Night; Khoya Khoya Chand*

Favourite Movie: *Anand, Godfather, Good Fellas*

Favourite Actor: Robert De Niro, Al Pacino

Favourite Female Actor: Sophia Loren

Acknowledgements

We thank all those people who have featured in this book and brought our story to life. We also thank all creative commons sources, from where information and images may have been used. We are grateful for all the cooperation extended to us in the making of this book by

Arup Raha - Air Chief Marshal (Retd)

Dr Sandip Chatterjee

Debal Banerjee

Sharmin Mukerjea

Shekhar Dutt - Former Governeor Chhattisgarh

Vice Chancellor Prof Saikat Maitra

Roger Taylor

Leander Paes

Sania Mirza

Jonathan Mermegan

Pradip Bajoria

Gaurav Misra

Bidyut Goswami

Anil Mukerji

Vece Paes

Praveen Singh

Nausher Madan

Rahul Basu

Rajit Pillai

Boria Majumdar

Gautam Bhattacharya

Saiful Islam

Shivaji Roy

Somenath Bose

Subhas Ganguly

Satyajit Burman

Murli Bhalotia

Rupinder Singh

Debanjan Chakraborty

Debonita Chakraborty

Vinoo Nath

Anamit Sen

Sudip Roy Choudhury

Prasun Roy

Sumit Roy

Debajyoti Banerjee

Somavo Gupta

Sunil (Laltu) Bhattacharya

Raj Dadich

Anup Chadda

Sunny Gayen

Vishnu Agarwal

Sushil Das

Debkumar Bandyopadhyay

Partha Ganguli

Bishnu Das (Bistu)

Bijay Das

Bhaswar Chakraborty

About Papri Sen Sri Raman

Papri Sen Sri Raman is a journalist editor, translator, biographer and writer. She is the winner of the third UNHCR C-NES Media Fellowship, 2008; Interpress Media Fellowship in 2008-09; The Kaiser Media Fellowship in 2007-08.

https://www.amazon.com.au/Jayalalithaa-PAPRI-SEN-SRI-RAMAN/dp/9382711864

https://www.amazon.in/Song-India-Papri-Sri-Raman/dp/9382711996

https://www.amazon.com/Spanish-Teacher-Papri-Sen-Raman/dp/1954021933